LEGAL RESEARCH, WRITING, AND ANALYSIS

SECOND EDITION

William P. Statsky
Antioch School of Law
Washington, D.C.

WEST PUBLISHING COMPANY
St. Paul   New York   Los Angeles   San Francisco

Library of Congress Cataloging in Publication Data

Statsky, William P.
    Legal research, writing, and analysis.
    Includes index.
    1. Legal research—United States.   I. Title.
KF240.S783   1982   340'.072073   82-2585
ISBN 0-314-65180-2   AACR2

4th Reprint—1985

CONTENTS

Chapter 1   LEGAL RESEARCH AND ANALYSIS   1

LEGAL RESEARCH, WRITING, AND ANALYSIS

Second Edition

Legal Research and Analysis

Section A. INTRODUCTION

This chapter does not cover every aspect of legal research nor does it treat every conceivable law book that could be found in a law library.   The chapter examines the components of legal research and analysis with the objective of identifying effective starting points.

When you walk into a law library, your first impression is likely to be that of awe.   You are confronted with row upon row of books, most of which seem unapproachable; they do not invite browsing.   To be able to use the law library, the first responsibility of the legal researcher is to break down any psychological barrier that you may have with respect to the books in it. This is done not only by learning the techniques of research, but also by understanding the limitations of the law library: what is the library capable of doing for you and what should you *not* ask it to do?

A major misunderstanding about the law library is that it contains the answer to every legal problem that confronts you as a researcher. As we shall see, in many instances, there are no definitive answers to legal problems. Very often the researcher operates on the basis of "educated guesses" of what the answer is. To be sure, your conclusions are often supported from what you uncover through legal research in the law library. The fact is, however, that the end product is only the researcher's opinion of what the law is, rather than the absolute answer. This is so because no one will know for sure what the "right" or final answer is until the matter is litigated in court. If the problem is never litigated, then the "right" answer will be whatever the parties accept among themselves, perhaps through negotiation or settlement. The researcher will not know what answer carries the day for the client in negotiation until the negotiation process begins. It is true, however, that there are many simple problems that can be answered by very basic (easy) legal research. If someone wants to know, for example, the name of the government agency in charge of incorporating a business or the maximum number of weeks one can receive unemployment compensation, finding the answer is not difficult if the researcher knows what books to go to and how to use the index to the books. Most legal research problems, however, are not this simple.

Perhaps the most healthy way to approach the law library is to view it not as a repository of answers, but as a storehouse of ambiguities that are waiting to be clarified, manipulated and applied to the facts of a client's case. You may have heard the story of a client who walked into a law office and asked to see a one-armed lawyer. When asked why he required an attorney meeting such specifications, he replied that he was tired of presenting problems to lawyers and having them constantly tell him that "on the one hand" he should do this, but "on the other hand" he should do that; he hungered for a lawyer who would give him an answer. This concern is well taken. A client is entitled to an answer, to clear guidance. At the same time, or, if you will, on the other hand, it is part of the lawyer's job to be weighing alternatives constantly, to be always thinking of options and counter-options, of the benefits and liabilities of any one particular course of action. The good lawyer is so inclined because s/he understands that our legal system is infested with unknowns and ambiguities. The good legal researcher also has this understanding. S/he is not frightened by ambiguities; s/he thrives on them.

Section B.   THE IMPORTANCE OF LEGAL RESEARCH

Lawyers and paralegals forget most of the law that they learn in school. And if they don't forget most of it, they should! No one can know all of the law at any given point in time, even in a specialty. Furthermore, the law is always changing. Nothing is more dangerous than someone walking around with out-of-date law. Law cannot be practiced on the basis of the rules one learned in school. Those rules cannot be relied upon since they may no longer be valid. Thousands of courts, legislatures and administrative agencies spend full time writing new laws and changing old ones.

The law library and the techniques of legal research are the indispensable tickets of admission to current law. School teaches you to think. *You teach yourself the law through the skill of legal research.* Everytime you walk into a law library, you are your own professor.   You must accept nothing less than to become an expert on the topic of your research no matter how narrow the topic is.   That is the purpose of the law library—to enable you to become an expert on the current law of your topic.   Do not fall into the trap of thinking that you must be an expert in an area of the law in order to research it properly.   The reverse is true.   A major way for you to become an expert in an area is through what you discover in the law library on your own.

You must never be reluctant to undertake legal research on a topic because you know very little about the topic.   Knowing very little is often the most healthy starting point for the researcher!   Preconceptions about the law can sometimes lead you away from avenues in the library that you should be traveling.

To become an expert through comprehensive legal research does not necessarily mean that you will know everything.   An expert is not simply someone who knows the answers; he or she is also someone who knows how to *formulate the questions that remain unanswered even after comprehensive legal research.*   An expert is someone who can say:

> *"This is what the current law says, and these are the questions that the law has not yet resolved."*

You cannot, of course, know what is unresolved until you know what is resolved.   The law library will tell you both.

Section C.   FRUSTRATION AND LEGAL RESEARCH

You are in the position of the king who sadly had to be told that there is no royal road to geometry.   If he wanted to learn geometry, he had to struggle through it like everyone else.   Legal research is a struggle and will remain so for the rest of your career.   The struggle will eventually become manageable and even enjoyable and exciting—but there is no way out of the struggle no matter how many short cuts you learn.   The amount of material in a law library is simply too massive for it to be otherwise, and again, the material is growing every day with new laws, new formats for law books, and new law publishers offering different services that must be mastered.   The first step in being able to handle the law library is to accept the fact that the struggle will never go away.

Unfortunately, many cannot handle the pressure that the law library seems to donate in abundance at times.   There are too many lawyers, for example, who stay away from the library and practice law "from the hip." Such lawyers need to be sure that they have extensive malpractice insurance!

Legal research will be difficult for you at the beginning, but with experience in the law library, the difficulties will become handleable.   The most important advice you can receive is: stick with it.   Spend a lot of time in the library.   Be inquisitive.   Ask a lot of questions of fellow students, teachers, librarians, lawyers and paralegals.   Be constantly on the alert for tips and techniques.   Take strange books from the shelf and try to figure out what they contain, what they try to do, how they are used and how they duplicate or complement other law books that are not strange to you.   Do not wait to be taught how to use sets of books that are new to you.   Strike out on your own.

The coming of computer technology to legal research is of some help, but the computers cannot eliminate your need to learn the basics. The struggle does not disappear if you are lucky enough to study or work where computers are available. Intelligent use of the computers requires an understanding of the fundamental techniques of legal research.

At this stage of your career, most of the frustration will center on the question of "how to begin your legal research of a topic." Once you master this problem, the concern will become, "how to end your legal research." Having located a great deal of material, you worry about when to stop. In this Chapter, we will discuss techniques of beginning. Techniques of stopping are more troublesome for the conscientious researcher. It is not always easy to determine whether you have found everything that you should find. While guidelines do exist and will be examined, it will take a great deal of experience with legal research before you can make the judgment that you have found everything that is available on a given topic. The important point is: don't be too hard on yourself. The techniques will come with time and practice. You will not learn everything now; you will only begin the learning that must continue throughout your career.

Always keep the following "laws" of legal research in mind:

1. *The only books that will be missing from a shelf are those that you need to use immediately.*
2. *The only sets of law books and legal research techniques that are worth learning are those that you will forget soon after learning them.*
3. *Each time you forget a technique, it will take you ½ less time to re-learn it than it took you the last time.*
4. *When you have re-learned it the fourth time, you own it.*

There will be times when you walk away from a set of law books after having used them and wonder what you have just done—even if you have gotten an answer from the books. There will be times when you will go back to a set of books that you have used before and draw a blank on what the books are and how to use them again. This is a natural occurrence. You will forget and you will forget again. Stay with it. Be willing to re-learn. You cannot master a set of books after using them only a few times. Learning legal research is a little like learning to play a musical instrument. There is a seat waiting for you in the orchestra, but you have got to practice! A royal road does not exist.

Section D. FLEXIBILITY IN LEGAL RESEARCH

Researchers have reached an enviable plateau when they understand the following paradox: researchers sometimes do not know what they are looking for until they find it. Since the simple answers are few and far between, researchers are constantly confronted with frustration and ambiguity. As they pursue avenues and leads, they invariably come upon new avenues and thoughts that never occurred to them initially. An entirely new approach to the problem may be uncovered which radically changes their initial perceptions. They reached this stage not because they consciously sought it out, but rather because they were flexible and open-minded enough to be receptive to new approaches and perceptions. This phenomenon is by no means peculiar to legal research.   Take the situation of the man in need of transportation.   He sets himself to the task of determining the most economical way to *buy* a good car.   In his search, he stumbles upon the practice of leasing cars.   After studying this option, he concludes that it would be the most sensible resolution of his problem of obtaining transportation.   He didn't know what he was looking for, a car *leasing* deal, until he found it.   Compare this to a client who comes into a law office for advice on how to write a will so that certain monies would pass to designated individuals upon death.   The lawyer asks you to do some legal research in the area of wills.   While in the law library studying the law of wills, you see reference to life insurance policies as a substitute for wills in passing cash to beneficiaries at death.   You bring this to the attention of the attorney who decides that it is indeed an option worth pursuing.   You did not know what you were looking for, a will substitute, until you found it.

Section E.   WRITE TO THE COMMERCIAL LAW PUBLISHERS

Below are a list of the major law publishers.   It is recommended that you write to each of them, particularly the ones with an asterisk (*) next to their names.   The investment in time and postage will be well worth it.   Send the same short note to each publisher:

"I would appreciate receiving a catalog of the law books you publish as well as any pamphlets you may have available on how to use your books.   Thank you."

Most publishers will respond (free of charge) with updated material describing their publications.   Have this material sent to your home address.   It may take several weeks before you receive a response.   When they send you the material, read it and compare what you read to what you will learn from this course.   The material will probably be of most use to you as a review rather than as introductory reading.

MAJOR COMMERCIAL LAW PUBLISHERS
(The most important are indicated by an asterisk*)

W. H. Anderson Co.
646 Main Street
Cincinnati, Ohio 45201

Matthew Bender & Co.
235 East 45th Street
New York, New York 10017

*Bureau of National Affairs
   (BNA)
1231 25th Street NW
Wash. D.C. 20037

Callaghan & Co.
3201 Old Glenview Road
Wilmette, Ill. 60091

Little Brown & Co.
Law Division
34 Beacon Street
Boston, Mass. 02106

Michie Co.
P.O. Box 7587
Charlottesville, Va. 22906

Prentice Hall
Englewood, New Jersey 07662

*Shepard's/McGraw-Hill
P.O. Box 1235
Colorado Springs, Colo. 80901

Clark Boardman Co.
435 Hudson Street
New York, New York 10014

Warren, Gorham & Lamont
210 South Street
Boston, Mass. 02111

*Commerce Clearing House
   (CCH)
4025 W. Peterson Ave.
Chicago, Ill. 60646

*West Publishing Co.
50 W. Kellogg Blvd.
P.O. Box 3526
St. Paul, Minn. 55102

Congressional Information
   Service (CIS)
7101 Wisconsin Ave. NW
Wash. D.C. 20014

John Wiley and Sons
605 Third Avenue
New York, New York 10016

*Lawyers Cooperative Publishing
   Co.
Aqueduct Bldg.
Rochester, New York 14603

Special Companies:

*Mead Data Central
200 Park Avenue
New York, New York 10166
(Ask for information on the LEXIS[1] computer)

*Information Access Corp.
404 Sixth Avenue
Menlo Park, Calif. 94025
(Ask for information on the Legal Resource Index[2] and the Current Law
Index[3])

*West Publishing Co.
(see address above)
(Ask for information on the WESTLAW℠[4] computer)

Section F.   THE VOCABULARY OF LEGAL RESEARCH: A CHECKLIST

This section consists of a list of 212 words and phrases, most of which
will be examined in the remainder of the chapter.   The list is the vocabulary
of legal research.   Before you are finished with this text, one of your goals
should be to know the meaning of everything on the list.   You must learn
to "talk" the language of legal research as well as "do" legal research.   Following each item in the list is a page number in parenthesis where it is covered
in the text.

ASSIGNMENT 1

For each of the words and phrases in the following list, prepare a 3 by
5 card on which you include the following information:

- the word or phrase
- the pages in this text where the word and phrase is discussed (begin with the page number in parenthesis below; add other page numbers as the words and phrases are discussed elsewhere in the text)
- the definition of the word or phrase and/or the function of the word or phrase and/or the list of the techniques or methods called for by the word or phrase
- other information about the word or phrase which you obtain as you use the materials or concepts referred to in the library
- comments by your instructor in class about any of the words and phrases

Some words and phrases will call for more than one card. You should strive, however, to keep the information on the cards brief.   Put the cards in alphabetical order.   The cards will become your own file system on legal research which you can use as a study guide for the course and as a reference tool as you are doing legal research in the library.   Be sure to add cards for words and phrases that are not on the following list as you come across new words and phrases in class and in your use of the library.

THE VOCABULARY OF LEGAL RESEARCH: A CHECKLIST

(The number in parenthesis refers to a page in the text.)

1. Act (11)
2. Acts and Resolves (13)
3. Administrative code (13)
4. Advance sheet, reporter (14)
5. Advance sheet, Shepard's (14)
6. ALR, ALR2d, ALR3d, ALR4th and ALR Fed (14)
7. ALR Blue Book of Supplemental Decisions (17)
8. ALR2 Digest (84)
9. ALR2d Later Case Service (86)
10. American Digest System (28)
11. American Law Institute (40)
12. Am Jur 2d (15)
13. Am Jur Pl & Pr Forms (109)
14. Am Jur Trials (109)
15. Am Jur Proof of Facts (109)
16. Amicus curiae brief (17)
17. Annotated reporter (15)
18. Annotation (15)
19. Appellant (115)
20. Appellate brief (17)
21. Appellate court (115)
22. Appellee (115)
23. Atlantic Digest (32)
24. Atlantic Reporter 2d (A.2d) (21)
25. Authority, mandatory (50)
26. Authority, persuasive (50)
27. Authority, primary (50)
28. Authority reference in CFR (138)
29. Authority, secondary (50)
30. Bill (16)
31. Blue Book (citations) (16)
32. BNA (18)
33. Brief of a case (118)
34. Brief of a statute (127)
35. Brackets in text of unofficial reporter (116)
36. California Reporter (Cal Rptr) (21)
37. Case (18)
38. Casebook (25)
39. Case on point (52)
40. CCH Congressional Index (130)
41. CCH U.S. Supreme Court Bulletin (18)
42. Century Digest (29)
43. Certiorari (cert)
44. Charter (11)
45. CARTWHEEL (70)
46. Citation (55)
47. Citator (25)
48. Cited material (Shepard's) (90)
49. Citing material (Shepard's) (90)
50. Code, Codify (26)
51. Code of Federal Regulations (CFR) (137)
52. Committee reports (129)
53. Common law (54)
54. Concurring opinion (118)
55. Congressional Information Service (CIS) (130)
56. Congressional Record (26)
57. Constitution (11)
58. Corpus Juris Secundum (CJS) (26)
59. Cumulative (27)
60. Cumulative Table of Key Numbers (in General Digest) (83)
61. Current Law Index (CLI) (106)
62. Decisions, administrative (11)
63. Decennial Digests (29)
64. Defendant-Plaintiff Table of Cases (in digests) (82)
65. Descriptive Word Index (of digests) (81)
66. Desk Book (rules of court) (41)
67. Dictum (118)
68. Digest (27)
69. Docket number (115)
70. Et seq. (100)
71. Executive order (11)
72. Federal Digest (30)
73. Federal Practice Digest 2d (30)
74. Federal Quick Index to Total-Client Service Library (85)
75. Federal Supplement (F.Supp.) (19)
76. Federal Register (33)
77. Federal Reporter 2d (F.2d) (19)
78. Federal Rules Decisions (F.R.D.) (19)
79. Formbook (34)
80. Forum (52)
81. General Digest (29)
82. Handbook (34)
83. Headnote (34)
84. Hornbook (35)
85. Index to Legal Periodicals (ILP) (105)
86. Index Medicus (107)
87. Interstate compact (35)
88. Key topic and number (27)
89. Key topic and number, four techniques for finding (81)
90. Law review (37)
91. Lawyers Co-operative Publishing Co. (Lawyers Co-op) (6)
92. Lawyers Edition (L.Ed.) (reporter) (18)
93. Legal dictionary (36)
94. Legal encyclopedia (36)
95. Legal newspaper (36)
96. Legal periodical literature (37)
97. Legal Resource Index (LRI) (106)
98. Legislative History (129)
99. LEXIS (112)
100. List of Parts Affected (in Federal Register) (138)
101. List of Sections Affected (LSA) (138)
102. Loose leaf service (103)
103. Majority opinion (118)
104. Martindale-Hubbell Law Directory (39)
105. MEDLINE (107)
106. Memorandum opinion (116)
107. Military Justice Reporter (20)
108. Modern Federal Practice Digest (30)
109. "n" found to the right of citing material in Shepard's (96)
110. National Reporter Blue Book (17)
111. National Reporter System (20)
112. New York Supplement (NYS) (21)
113. Nominative reporters (60)
114. Non-authority (51)
115. North Eastern 2d (N.E.2d) (22)
116. North Western Digest (32)
117. North Western 2d (N.W.2d) (22)
118. Notes of decisions (123)
119. Official citation (57)
120. On point (51)
121. Opinion (11)
122. Opinion of the Attorney General (11)

Section G.   FINDING LAW LIBRARIES

First things first.   Before learning how to do legal research, you must have access to a law library.   Since it is rare that you will be able to find everything you need in a single library, it would be more accurate to say that you must know how to locate the variety of law libraries that are potentially available to you.   It is not uncommon for the precise law book you need to be missing from the shelf of an otherwise comprehensive library.   It is not uncommon for even a large library to fail to subscribe to a set of books that you need or to be out of date on a set of books that you must use.   Finally, it is not uncommon for you to have such particular legal research needs that you must search for specialized collections of books.

The availability of law libraries depends to a large degree on the area in which you live, work and study.   Rural areas will have fewer possibilities than large cities or capitals.   Furthermore, some libraries may be open to you only with special permission.

You begin, of course, with the library where you are a student.   Hopefully, it will meet most of your research needs.   Visit the law librarian as soon as possible.   Ask this person if s/he has a list or directory of law libraries or librarians in your city.   Ask your law librarian which libraries are open to the public and which require special permission for use.   Also ask for suggestions on obtaining this permission.

The following is a list of possible libraries in your area with suggestions on how to gain access:

1. Law School Libraries
   - ask students who attend the school if it is open to outsiders
   - ask the librarian or the dean of the school if you can use the facilities
   - ask your own librarian or dean to contact the other school on your behalf
2. Paralegal School Libraries
   - same suggestions as above
3. State Law Libraries
   - ask a lawyer who uses the library for help in gaining access
   - ask a local politician's office to help you
   - ask the state law librarian for permission
   - ask your own librarian or dean to seek permission on your behalf
4. Law Libraries in the Legislature
   - ask your legislator for help
   - ask the librarian in the legislature's law library
   - ask your own librarian or dean to seek permission on your behalf
5. Law Libraries of Administrative Agencies (e.g., worker's compensation agency, human services agency)
   - ask the director of the agency for permission
   - ask staff lawyers or paralegals who work at the agency for help
   - ask a local politician's office for help
   - ask a staff member of the agency's library
   - ask your own librarian or dean to seek permission on your behalf
6. Bar Association Law Libraries
   - ask a member of the association if you can be his/her guest in the library
   - contact the president of the association for help
   - ask the association's law librarian
   - ask your own librarian or dean to make the contact on your behalf
7. The Law Libraries of Other Associations (e.g., insurance companies, real estate agents, unions)
   - ask a member of the association if s/he can sponsor your use of the library
   - contact the president of the association for help
   - contact the association's librarian
   - ask your own librarian or dean to make the contact on your behalf
8. Public Interest Law Office Libraries (e.g., a legal service office, a conservation or environmental law office)
   - ask a staff lawyer or paralegal for help
   - ask the director of the office
   - ask the librarian of the office's library
   - ask your own librarian or dean to make the contact on your behalf
9. The Law Office of the Attorney General or Corporation Counsel
   - ask a staff attorney or paralegal for help
   - ask a local politician's office for help
   - ask the law librarian there for permission
   - ask the attorney general or the corporation counsel for permission
   - ask your own librarian or dean to make the contact for you

10. The Law Library of Courts
    - ask the librarian at the court for permission
    - ask the judge for permission
    - ask your own librarian or dean to make the contact for you
11. The Law Library of Private Law Firms
    - ask a lawyer or paralegal at the firm for help
    - ask the firm's librarian
    - ask your librarian or dean to make the contact for you

In short, you will have to use some ingenuity to locate these libraries and to gain access to them.   Try more than one avenue of entry.   Some libraries might be willing to let you use the facilities in exchange for several hours of volunteer work in the library.   Don't get discouraged when the first person you contact tells you that the library is for members only.   There are some students who adopt the strategy of walking into any library and acting as if they belong.   Rather than ask for permission, they wait for someone to stop them or to question their right to be there.   Other students take the wiser course of seeking permission in advance.   Yet, even here, some creativity is needed in the way that you ask for permission.   The bold question, "Can I use your library?" may be less effective than an approach such as, "Would it be possible for me to use some of your law books for a short period of time for some important research that I must do?"

Section H.   A GLOSSARY OF LAW AND LAW BOOKS: INTRODUCTION

There are approximately ten categories of law which you should know. The purpose of legal research is to find these laws, to check their current validity and to apply them to the facts of the research problem.   Step one is to know the definitions of the categories.

A word of caution in approaching the vocabulary of law and legal research: often the same word or phrase can have a different meaning depending upon the context in which it is used.   "Supreme Court," for example, refers to the highest court in our federal judicial system as well as to the trial court in New York State, and the word, "opinion" refers both to administrative decisions of agencies and to the judicial decisions of courts.   While there are definitions that are generally used, you should be prepared to find variations. (See the chart on page 11, "Kinds of Law.")

Next we will begin examining the sets of books in the library which are relevant to the above categories of laws.   For each category of law, four kinds of books should be kept in mind:

1. Sets of books that contain the full text of the law.
2. Sets of books that can be used to locate that kind of law.
3. Sets of books that can be used to help explain that kind of law.
4. Sets of books that can be used to help determine the current validity of that kind of law.

Some sets of books serve more than one of the above four functions.   The chart beginning on page 12 presents an overview of law books according to the above functions.   After the chart, descriptions and definitions of the major sets of books in the chart will be provided.

Kinds of Law

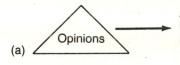

(a) Opinions

An *opinion* (sometimes called a *case*) is the explanation by a court of why it reached a certain decision on the application of law to the specific facts before the court.

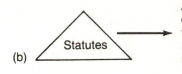

(b) Statutes

A *statute* is a law or act passed by the legislature declaring, commanding or prohibiting something. An *act* is the document that contains the statute. *Public statutes* apply to the public generally. *Private statutes* apply to specific individuals or groups.

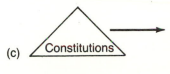

(c) Constitutions

A *constitution* is the fundamental law which creates the branches of government and identifies basic rights and obligations.

(d) Administrative Regulations

An *administrative regulation* (sometimes called a *rule*) is a law of an administrative agency designed to explain and carry out the statutes or executive orders that govern the agency.

(e) Administrative Decisions

An *administrative decision* (sometimes called an *opinion* or *ruling*) is a resolution of a specific controversy involving the application of the agency's regulations or its governing statutes and executive orders.

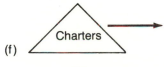

(f) Charters

A *charter* is the fundamental law of a municipality or other local unit of government authorizing it to perform designated governmental functions.

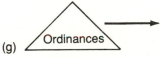

(g) Ordinances

An *ordinance* is a law passed by the local legislative branch of government, e.g., city council, county commission.

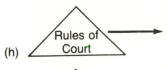

(h) Rules of Court

Rules of court (sometimes called *court rules* or *rules of procedure*) are the laws governing practice before a particular court and the procedures to be followed in litigation before that court.

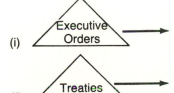

(i) Executive Orders

An *executive order* is a law issued by the chief executive to direct the operation of governmental agencies.

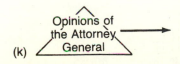

(j) Treaties

A *treaty* is an international agreement entered into between two or more countries.

(The following falls into a separate category. They are advisory and hence are not considered laws in the same sense as the above ten.)

(k) Opinions of the Attorney General

An *opinion of the attorney general* (sometimes called an opinion of the *corporation counsel*) is legal advice given by the attorney general to government officials on legal issues such as the interpretation of a statute.

KINDS OF LAW BOOKS: A CHECKLIST

KIND OF LAW	SETS OF BOOKS THAT CONTAIN THE FULL TEXT OF THIS KIND OF LAW	SETS OF BOOKS THAT CAN BE USED TO LOCATE THIS KIND OF LAW	SETS OF BOOKS THAT CAN BE USED TO HELP EXPLAIN THIS KIND OF LAW	SETS OF BOOKS THAT CAN BE USED TO HELP DETERMINE THE CURRENT VALIDITY OF THIS KIND OF LAW
(a) Opinions	Reports Reporters ALR, ALR2d, ALR3d, ALR4th, ALR Fed Legal newspapers Loose leaf services Slip opinion Advance sheets	Digests Annotations in ALR, ALR2d, ALR3d, ALR4th, ALR Fed Shepard's Legal periodicals Encyclopedias Treatises Loose leaf services Words and Phrases	Legal periodicals Encyclopedias Treatises Annotations in ALR, ALR2d, ALR3d, ALR4th, ALR Fed Loose leaf services	Shepard's
(b) Statutes	Statutory Code Statutes Statutes at Large Session Laws Laws Compilations Consolidated Laws Slip Law Acts, Acts & Resolves	Index volumes of statutory code Loose leaf services	Legal periodicals Encyclopedias Treatises Annotations in ALR, ALR2d, ALR3d, ALR4th, ALR Fed Loose leaf services	Shepard's
(c) Constitutions	Statutory code Separate volumes containing the constitution	Index volumes of statutory code Loose leaf services	Legal periodicals Encyclopedias Treatises Annotations in ALR, ALR2d, ALR3d, ALR4th, ALR Fed Loose leaf services	Shepard's
(d) Administrative Regulations	Administrative Codes Separate volumes or pamphlets containing the regulations of certain agencies Loose leaf services	Index volumes of the administrative code Loose leaf services	Legal periodicals Treatises Annotations in ALR, ALR2d, ALR3d, ALR4th, ALR Fed Loose leaf services	Shepard's (for some agencies only)
(e) Administrative Decisions	Separate volumes of decisions of certain agencies Loose leaf services	Loose leaf services Index or digest volumes to the decisions	Legal periodicals Treatises Annotations in ALR, ALR2d, ALR3d, ALR4th, ALR Fed Loose leaf services	Shepard's (for some agencies only)
(f) Ordinances	Municipal code Official journal Legal newspaper	Index volumes of municipal code	Legal periodicals Treatises Annotations in ALR, ALR2d, ALR3d, ALR4th, ALR Fed	Shepard's
(g) Charters	Separate volumes containing the charter Municipal Code State session laws Official journal Legal newspaper	Index volumes to the charter or municipal code	Legal periodicals Treatises Annotations in ALR, ALR2d, ALR3d, ALR Fed	Shepard's
(h) Rules of Court	Separate rules volumes Statutory code Practice manuals	Index to separate rules volumes Index to statutory code Index to practice manuals	Practice manuals Treatises Annotations in ALR, ALR2d, ALR3d ALR4th, ALR Fed Encyclopedias Loose leaf services	Shepard's
(i) Executive Orders	Federal Register Code of Federal Regulations U.S. Code Congressional and Administrative News USC, USCA, USCS (for some orders only)	Index volumes to the sets of books listed in the second column	Legal periodicals Treatises Annotations in ALR, ALR2d, ALR3d, ALR4th, ALR Fed	Shepard's Code of Federal Regulation Citations
(j) Treaties	Statutes at Large (up to 1950) United States Treaties and Other International Agree-	Index within the volumes listed in second column	Legal periodicals Treatises Annotations in ALR, ALR2d, ALR3d, ALR 4th, ALR Fed	Shepard's (for some treaties only)

KINDS OF LAW BOOKS—continued

KINDS OF LAW BOOKS—continued

	ments Department of State Bulletin Treaties in Force			
(k) Opinions of the Attorney Gen- eral	Separate volumes containing these opinions	Digests Index in separate volumes of the opinions		

The following is a description of some of the major legal research terms including many used in the above chart:

ACTS; ACTS AND RESOLVES

An act is the official document that contains the statute passed by the legislature.   Acts and Resolves is the set of books that contain all the acts of the legislature.   They are also sometimes called Session Laws (see this entry below), Statutes (see this entry), Statutes at Large (see this entry), Laws, etc. A major characteristic of all of these books is that they print the statutes of the legislature chronologically as they are passed.   They are not classified or organized by subject matter.   (See entry on Code.)

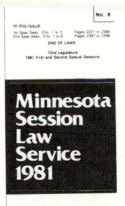

ADMINISTRATIVE CODE

An administrative code is a collection of the regulations of an agency organized by subject matter.   Not all states have such codes.   Generally, the regulations of state and local administrative agencies are poorly organized and difficult to obtain.   Not so with the federal agencies:

Code of Federal Reguluations (CFR) containing many of the regulations of federal agencies, e.g., U.S. Department of Agriculture.

ADVANCE SHEET

An advance sheet is a pamphlet printed before (in "advance" of) a bound volume or before a thicker pamphlet which will consolidate the material in several of the earlier advance sheets. When the bound volume or thicker pamphlet comes out, the advance sheet is thrown away. There are two kinds of advance sheets in the law library: an advance sheet for reporters and one for Shepard's.

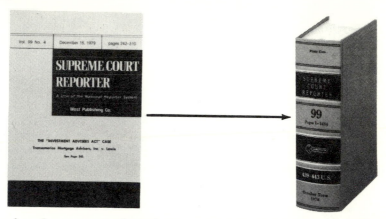

Advance sheet for a reporter (here the Supreme Court Reporter). The advance sheet contains the full text of court opinions that will later be printed in a bound Supreme Court Reporter volume.

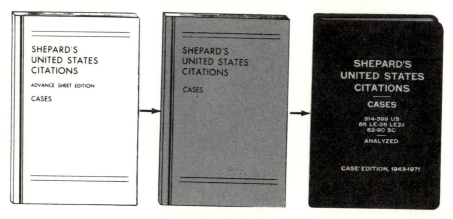

Advance sheet for Shepard's (here United States Citations, Cases covering cases of the U.S. Supreme Court). The advance contains the "shepardizing" data that will be printed later in thicker pamphlets and eventually into bound Shepard's volumes.

ALR, ALR2d, ALR3d, ALR4th, ALR Fed

ALR:	American Law Reports, First Series
ALR2d:	American Law Reports, Second Series
ALR3d:	American Law Reports, Third Series
ALR4th:	American Law Reports, Fourth Series
ALR Fed:	American Law Reports, Federal Series

These sets of books contain the complete text of *selected* court opinions followed by extensive commentary or research papers on issues within the opinions selected. These research papers are called annotations (see this entry). The sets of books are therefore called annotated reports. The annotations are excellent case finders.

American
Law Reports,
Third Series

AMERICAN JURISPRUDENCE 2d

Am Jur 2d is a national legal encyclopedia (published by Lawyers Co-operative Publishing Co.) which provides numerous discussions/summaries of almost every area of the law. It is very useful (a) as background reading before beginning legal research on a topic and (b) as a case finder because of the extensive footnotes. (Am Jur 2d is the second edition of Am Jur First.) Its competitor is Corpus Juris Secundum (see this entry).

ANNOTATION

To annotate something means to provide critical notes or commentary. An annotated bibliography, for example, is a list of references (citations) plus brief summaries or comments on each entry on the list.[5] An "annotated report" is the full text of a court opinion plus notes or commentary on the opinion or a part of it. The word "annotation" refers to the notes and commentary that follow the opinions found in ALR, ALR2d, ALR3d, ALR4th, and ALR Fed (see this entry). You are being directed to these sets of books when someone asks you to "find out if there are any annotations on this point." The phrase "annotated code" or "annotated statutes" are also sometimes used, e.g., United States Code Annotated. Annotated codes or statutes refer to sets of statutes that contain the full text of the statutes plus similar kinds of research references. The abbreviation for annotation is usually "ann.", e.g., Del. Code Ann.

AMERICAN DIGEST SYSTEM

See Digest.

ATLANTIC DIGEST

See Digest.

ATLANTIC REPORTER 2d (A.2d)

See Cases.

BALLENTINE'S LAW DICTIONARY

See Legal Dictionary.

BILL

A bill is a proposed statute, i.e., one that has not yet been enacted into law. Bills are printed in small booklet or pamphlet form. Federal bills are also printed in the Congressional Record (see this entry).

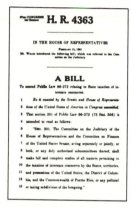

BLACK'S LAW DICTIONARY

See Legal Dictionary.

BLUE BOOK

The phrase "blue book" will usually refer to one of the three following books or sets of books:

- Uniform System of Citation
- National Reporter Blue Book
- ALR Blue Book of Supplemental Decisions

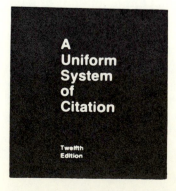

Uniform System of Citation.   A small pamphlet published by the law reviews of several law schools.   The pamphlet covers the "rules" of citation form.   It is considered by many to be the bible of citation form. (See Citation.)

National Reporter Blue Book.   A set of books published by West that will enable you to find a parallel cite to a court opinion.

Finally, the *ALR Blue Book of Supplemental Decisions* will enable you to update the annotations found in **ALR First Series** (see p. 86 infra).

BRIEF

A brief is a written document prepared by a party for submission to an appellate court in which arguments are presented on the correctness or incorrectness of what the trial court did or failed to do.   It is called an appellate brief.

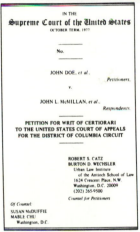

Amicus Curiae means friend of the court.   An *amicus curiae* brief is also an appellate brief, but it is prepared and submitted by a non-party.   A court must give permission for a non-party to submit such a brief.

It is often possible for you to locate appellate briefs written on recent cases.   They can provide excellent research leads for current cases on which you are working for similar issues.[6]

The word "brief" is also used in two other senses.   First, a trial brief (sometimes called a trial manual or trial book) is a collection of all the documents, arguments and strategies that an attorney plans to use at trial.   It is his/her blueprint for conducting the trial.   Second, a brief of a case (court opinion) is your own notes on the case including the key facts of the case, the issues in the case, the reasoning of the court, the disposition, etc.[7]

BULLETIN

The word Bulletin is used to describe a number of different law books.   Law reviews or bar journals, for example, sometimes use this word as part of their title. (See Legal Periodical.) Some administrative agencies publish documents pertaining to the work of their agencies in what are called Bulletins.

CALIFORNIA REPORTER (CAL.RPTR.)

See Cases.

CASES

The word case is often used interchangeably with the word opinion. The full text of cases are found in volumes called reports or reporters. An official reporter is printed by the government. An unofficial reporter is printed by a private publishing company (mainly West). First we will examine the reporters containing opinions of the federal courts. Then we will look at the reporters for state courts.

Federal Court Opinions

The opinions of the United States Supreme Court are printed in an official report, United States Reports (abbreviated "U.S."), and by several unofficial reporters: the Supreme Court Reporter published by West (abbreviated "S.Ct.") and United States Supreme Court Reports, Lawyers' Edition published by Lawyer's Co-operative Company (abbreviated "L.Ed."). "Official" simply means printed by the government itself.

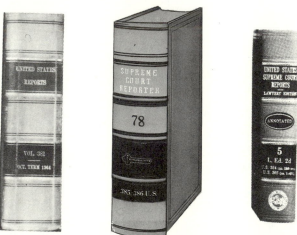

There are two loose leaf services (see this entry) that also print the full text of all U.S. Supreme Court opinions:

1. United States Law Week (USLW) published by Bureau of National Affairs (BNA)
2. United States Supreme Court Bulletin published by Commerce Clearing House (CCH)

There are four major reporters that contain the full text of opinions from the lower federal courts:

1. Federal Reporter (abbreviated "F.")
   Federal Reporter, Second Series (abbreviated "F.2d")

2. Federal Supplement (abbreviated "F. Supp.")
3. Federal Rules Decisions (abbreviated "F.R.D.")
4. Military Justice Reporter (abbreviated "M.J.")

These are all unofficial reporters since they are published by West, a private company.

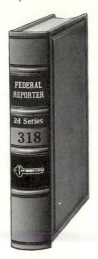

1. **Federal Reporter, Second Series (F.2d).**   Currently contains the full text of the opinions written by the following courts: United States Courts of Appeal, United States Court of Claims, United States Court of Customs and Patent Appeals.

2. **Federal Supplement (F.Supp.).**   Currently contains the full text of the opinions written by the United States District Courts and the United States Custom Court.

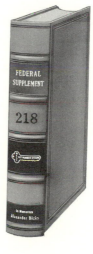

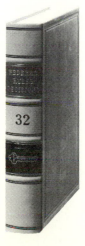

3. **Federal Rules Decisions (F.R.D.).**   Currently contains the full text of the opinions written by the United States District Courts (limited to opinions interpreting the federal rules of civil and criminal procedure, when such opinions are not printed in the F. Supp. reporter).

4. Military Justice Reporter (M.J.).   Currently contains the full text of opinions written by the United States Court of Military Appeals.

State Court Opinions

At one time all states had official reports of their highest state courts.   An example of an official state report:

     Recently, however, many states began discontinuing their official reports. For such states, the unofficial reports of the opinions are all that exist.   The major publisher of unofficial state reports is West through its National Reporter System.   The National Reporter System is a series of fourteen unofficial reporters containing the full text of opinions from the courts covered in the reporters.   We have already looked at the five reporters of the National Reporter System that contain *federal* court opinions:

- Supreme Court Reporter
- Federal Reporter (First and Second)
- Federal Supplement
- Federal Rules Decisions
- Military Justice Reporter

We now look at the remaining nine reporters of the System which contain the full (unofficial text) of *state* court opinions:

The following reporters currently contain the full text of the opinions written by the courts indicated next to the reporter:

Atlantic Reporter (A.), Atlantic Reporter, Second Series (A.2d).   The opinions of the highest state court in the following states: Conn., Del., Maine, Maryland, N.H., N.J., Penn., R.I., Vt., plus the District of Columbia.

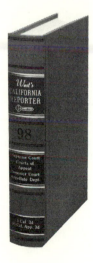

California Reporter (Cal. Rptr.).   The opinions of the highest Court of California as well as many opinions of the lower state courts in California.

New York Supplement (N.Y.S.), New York Supplement, Second (N.Y.S.2d).   The opinions of the highest state court in New York as well as many opinions of the lower state courts in New York.

North Eastern Reporter (N.E.), North Eastern Reporter, Second (N.E.2d).   The opinions of the highest state court in the following states: Ill., Ind., Mass., N.Y., Ohio.

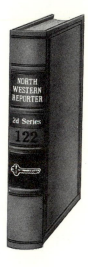

North Western Reporter (N.W.), North Western Reporter, Second Series (N.W.2d).   The opinions of the highest state court in the following states: Iowa, Mich., Minn., Neb., N.D., S.D., Wisc.

Pacific Reporter (P.), Pacific Reporter, Second Series (P.2d).   The opinions of the highest state court in the following states: Alaska, Ariz., Cal., Colo., Hawaii, Idaho, Kan., Mont., Nev., N.M., Okla., Ore., Utah, Wash., Wyo.

South Eastern Reporter (S.E.), South Eastern Reporter, Second Series (S.E.2d). The opinions of the highest state court in the following states: Ga., N.C., S.C., Va., W.Va.

Southern Reporter (S.), Southern Reporter, Second Series (S.2d). The opinions of the highest state court in the following states: Ala., Fla., La., Miss.

South Western Reporter (S.W.), South Western Reporter, Second Series (S.W.2d). The opinions of the highest state courts in the following states: Ark., Ky., Mo., Tenn., Tex.

Seven of the above reporters are called *regional* reporters since they contain the full text of opinions from states in a designated region of the country. These seven regional reporters can be seen on the following map:

NATIONAL REPORTER SYSTEM MAP

Showing the States included in each Reporter group

	Pacific
	North Western
	South Western
	North Eastern
	Atlantic
	South Eastern
	Southern

If a law office subscribes to a regional reporter from West, the office is obviously receiving the opinions from states in addition to its own. West also publishes special state editions for most of the states. These special edition state reporters contain only the opinions of an individual state that are also printed in the regional reporter. For example, you saw above that the opinions of the highest court in Kansas are printed in the Pacific Reporter. A Kansas lawyer who does not want to subscribe to the Pacific Reporter can subscribe to the special edition Kansas reporter called Kansas cases.

A volume of Kansas Cases (a special edition state reporter) containing all the Kansas opinions printed in Pacific Reporter, 2d.

Major Characteristics of West Reporters

- Contains the full text of court opinions
- The opinions are arranged in rough chronological order
- The reporters have advance sheets that come out before the bound volumes
- There are Table of Cases at the beginning of each reporter volume
- There is a Table of Statutes Construed in many reporters listing the statutes interpreted within the individual reporter volume
- There is *no* subject-matter index in any individual reporter volume (the main index to the opinions in reporters is the separate set of books called digests (see this entry)
- Every opinion in the reporter is broken down into small paragraph summaries called headnotes (see this entry and Digests). These headnotes are printed at the beginning of the individual opinion.

CASEBOOK

A casebook is a law school textbook which is mainly a collection of court opinions and other materials relating to a particular area of the law, e.g., Lockhart, Kamisar and Choper, *Constitutional Rights and Liberties: Cases and Materials* (1975).

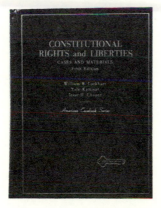

CENTURY DIGEST

See Digest.

CITATION

A citation (also called a cite) is a reference to any written material, e.g., a case, statute, law review article, treatise, annotation, report. The reference tells you how to locate the item, e.g., volume number, name of book, edition, page number, section number. A complete cite gives all the information required by proper citation form. A parallel cite is an additional reference to the *exact same* item. If there are two parallel cites to a case, for example, you will be able to find the same case—word for word—in two different reporters.[8] A book on citation form is the Uniform System of Citation (see Blue Book).

CITATOR

A citator is simply a book containing lists of cites. The major citator in legal research is Shepard's. The columns of Shepard's contain nothing but citations that are relevant to whatever you are "shepardizing." (See Shepard's)

CODE

A code is a collection of laws or rules classified by subject-matter. To codify something means to re-arrange it by subject matter. The arrangement of uncodified material is chronological as it is created; the arrangement of codified material is by topic. When statutes are first passed by the legislature, they are placed in uncodified books called sessions laws, acts and resolves, statutes at large, etc. Most of these statutes are later codified into statutory codes. (See Statutory Code) Regulations are also sometimes codified. (See Administrative Code)

CODE OF FEDERAL REGULATIONS (C.F.R.)

See Administrative Code.

CONGRESSIONAL RECORD

An official collection of the day-to-day happenings of Congress. The Congressional Record is one source of legislative history[9] for federal statutes. It also contains many items that are only relevant to the districts of individual legislators.

CORPUS JURIS SECUNDUM

Corpus Juris Secundum (CJS) is a national legal encyclopedia (published by West) which provides numerous discussions/summaries of almost every area of the law. It is very useful (a) as background reading before beginning legal research on a topic and (b) as a case finder because of the extensive footnotes. Its competitor is American Jurisprudence 2d (see this entry)

CUMULATIVE

Cumulative means that which consolidates earlier material. A cumulative supplement, for example, is a pamphlet or volume that up-dates and con-solidates all earlier pamphlets or volumes. The earlier material can be thrown away. Similarly, pocket parts[10] (containing supplemental material at the end of a book) often are cumulative. When the most recent pocket part comes out, the old one can be thrown away.

DECENNIAL DIGEST

See Digest.

DIGESTS

Our goals in this section are to define digest, to identify the major digests, and to explain the relationship between digests and reporters. Later in the chapter, we will cover the techniques of using digests in research.[11]

Digests are volumes containing small paragraph summaries of court opinions organized by subject matter. Their primary purpose is to serve as case finders. The major publisher of digests is West. Its *key number system* is the organizational principle used to classify the small paragraph summaries of the opinions in the digests. Every topic and sub-topic in the law is assigned a key topic and number by West. For example:

> 290. Strikes and lockouts.
>
> 984. Sentence on conviction on dif-ferent counts.
>
> 406.3(9). Clearly erroneous findings of court or jury.

Once you find a key topic (and sub-topic) plus its key number relevant to your research problem, you are given the paragraph summaries of cases under that topic and number. For example, the following are cases digested under the topic of "obscenity" and the sub-topics of "Nature and elements of offenses in general" and "Statutory provisions":

OBSCENITY

🗝1. **Nature and elements of offenses in general.**

Ill.App. 1973. Obscenity vel non is not constitutionally protected. People v. Rota, 292 N.E.2d 738.

Iowa 1973. Knowledge of obscene material is an essential element in obscenity prosecutions. I.C.A. § 725.5. State v. Lavin, 204 N.W.2d 844.

🗝2. **Statutory provisions.**

D.C.Md. 1972. Although Maryland motion picture censorship statute did not provide disseminator of motion picture film with an adversary hearing before board of censors on issue of obscenity, disseminator was not constitutionally prejudiced in this regard because the statute requires an adversary judicial determination of obscenity with circuit court for Baltimore City exercising de novo review of the board's finding of obscenity, and with burden of proving that the film is unprotected expression resting on the board. Code Md. 1957, art. 66A, §§ 6(c, d), 19(a); 28 U.S.C.A. § 100. Star v. Preller, 352 F.Supp. 530.

Notice the citations to the cases that follow each paragraph summary, e.g., People v. Rota in the first paragraph listed.

There are a few digests that are not published by West, e.g., the United States Supreme Court Digest, L.Ed. published by Lawyers Co-operative Publishing Company. These digests also contain small paragraph summaries of court opinions, but since they are not published by West, they are not organized by the key topic system. They use their own organization principle.

What are the digests that exist? Four main kinds can be identified:

- A national digest covering most state and federal appellate courts and some lower state and federal courts
- Federal digests covering all federal courts
- Regional digests covering the courts found in the regional reporters
- Digests of individual courts or states

National Digest

There is one national digest—the American Digest System published by West. It contains small paragraph summaries of the court opinions of most state and federal appellate courts and some lower state and federal courts. The American Digest System has three main units: Century Digest, Decennial Digest, and General Digest.

(a) A sample volume from the Century Digest, covering summaries of opinions written between 1658 and 1896.

(b) The decennial digests cover summaries of opinions for ten year periods starting in 1897.   A sample volume from the Eighth Decennial covering the ten year period from 1966–1976.

(c) The general digest covering summaries of opinions since the last decennial was published.   When the current ten year period is over, all the general digests will be thrown away, since the summaries within them will be consolidated into the next decennial.

Federal Digests Covering All Federal Courts

There are three main digests that cover all the federal courts, e.g., the U.S. Supreme Court, the U.S. Courts of Appeal, the U.S. District Courts.   These three digests are distinguished primarily by the years that they cover:

Federal Digest contains small paragraph summaries of federal cases decided up to 1939.

Modern Federal Practice Digest contains small paragraph summaries of federal cases decided between 1939 and 1961.

Modern Federal Practice Digest 2d contains small paragraph summaries of federal cases decided from 1962 to the present.

Regional Digests

Regional digests contain small paragraph summaries of court opinions printed in full in its corresponding regional reporter. The opinions in the Pacific Reporter, for example, are digested in the Pacific Digest:

As we shall see in the chart below, not all regional reporters have their own regional digest.   (There is no regional digest for the North Eastern Reporter and for the South Western Reporter.   The other five regional reporters have corresponding regional digests.)

Digests of Individual Courts or States

Some digests cover only certain courts.   There are two digests, for example, that cover only the United States Supreme Court:

United States Supreme Court Digest.   Published by West containing small paragraph summaries of every opinion of the U.S. Supreme Court.

United States Supreme Court Digest, L.Ed.   Published by Lawyers Cooperative Publishing Company containing small paragraph summaries of every opinion of the U.S. Supreme Court.

A state digest contains small paragraph summaries of the opinions of the state courts within that state as well as the opinions of the federal courts that are relevant to that state.   The following are examples of state digests:

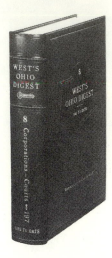

Now let us summarize.   In the following chart, there is a list of reporters, the names of the courts whose full opinions are printed in that reporter and the names of the digests that give small paragraph summaries of those opinions.

REPORTERS AND DIGESTS: A CHECKLIST		
NAME OF REPORTER	THE COURTS WHOSE OPINIONS ARE PRINTED IN FULL IN THIS RE-PORTER	THE DIGESTS THAT CONTAIN SMALL PARAGRAPH SUMMARIES OF THE OPINIONS IN THIS REPORTER
United States Reports (U.S.) Supreme Court Reporter (S.Ct.) United States Supreme Court Reports, Lawyers' Edition (L.Ed.) United States Law Week (U.S.L.W.) United States Supreme Court Bulletin (CCH)	United States Supreme Court	American Digest System United States Supreme Court Digest (West) United States Supreme Court Digest, L.Ed. Federal Digest (up to 1939) Modern Federal Practice Digest (1939–1961) Modern Federal Practice Digest, 2d (1962–present) Individual state digests (for Supreme Court cases relevant to that state)
Federal Reporter, 2d (F.2d)	United States Courts of Appeal United States Court of Claims United States Court of Customs and Patent Appeals	American Digest System Federal Digest (up to 1939) Modern Federal Practice Digest (1939–1961) Modern Federal Practice Digest, 2d (1962–present) Individual state digests (for federal cases relevant to that state)
Federal Supplement (F.Supp.)	United States District Courts United States Custom Court	American Digest System Federal Digest (up to 1939) Modern Federal Practice Digest (1939–1961) Modern Federal Practice Digest, 2d (1962–present) Individual state digests (for federal cases relevant to that state)
Atlantic Reporter 2d (A.2d)	The highest state court in Conn., Del., Maine, Md., N.H., N.J., Pa., R.I., Vt., District of Columbia	American Digest System Atlantic Digest Individual state digests
North Eastern Reporter, 2d (N.E.2d)	The highest state court in Ill., Ind., Mass., N.Y., Ohio	American Digest System Individual state digests (There is *no* North Eastern Digest)
North Western Reporter, 2d (N.W.2d)	The highest state court in Iowa, Mich., Minn., Neb., N.D., S.D., Wisc.	American Digest System North Western Digest Individual state digests
Pacific Reporter, 2d (P.2d)	The highest state court in Alaska, Ariz., Cal., Colo., Hawaii, Idaho, Kan., Mont., Nev., N.M., Okla., Ore., Utah, Wash., Wyo.	American Digest System Pacific Digest Individual state digests

REPORTERS AND DIGESTS—continued

REPORTERS AND DIGESTS—continued

South Eastern Reporter, 2d (S.E.2d)	The highest state court in Ga., N.C., S.C., Va., W.Va.	American Digest System South Eastern Digest Individual state digests
Southern Reporter, 2d (S.2d)	The highest state court in Ala., Fla., La., Miss.	American Digest System Southern Digest Individual state digests
South Western Reporter, 2d (S.W.2d)	The highest state court in Ark., Ky., Mo., Tenn., Tex.	American Digest System Individual state digests (There is *no* South Western Digest)

FEDERAL CASES

The name of the reporter (see Cases) that contains very early opinions of the federal courts (up to 1880) before F.2d and F.Supp. began.

FEDERAL DIGEST

See Digests.

FEDERAL PRACTICE DIGEST 2d

See Digests.

FEDERAL REGISTER (F.R.)

The Federal Register is a daily publication of the federal government which prints: proposed regulations of the federal administrative agencies; executive orders and other executive documents; news from federal agencies, e.g., announcements calling for applications for federal grants, etc.   Many of the regulations that are adopted by the federal agencies are later printed in the Code of Federal Regulations (C.F.R.) (see Administrative Code).

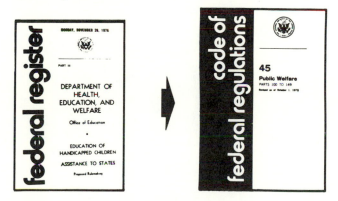

FEDERAL RULES DECISIONS (F.R.D.)

See Cases.

FEDERAL SUPPLEMENT

See Cases.

FEDERAL REPORTER

See Cases.

FORMBOOK

A formbook is a manual written by private individuals giving practical information on how to practice law in a given area.   It contains summaries of the law, checklists, sample forms, etc.   They are how-to-do-it texts.   Formbooks can be single or multi-volume.   Other names for formbooks are *practice manuals, handbooks,* etc.   Examples of formbooks:

GENERAL DIGEST

See Digest.

HANDBOOK

A formbook (see this entry).

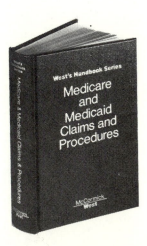

HEADNOTE

A headnote is a summary of a portion of an opinion printed just before the opinion begins.   In West reporters (see Cases), each headnote is numbered consecutively and is assigned a key topic and number.   The headnote is later also printed in the digests of West (see Digests).

> **3. Libel and Slander** ⌐⊃28
>
> Since one may not escape liability for dafamation by showing that he was merely repeating defamatory language used by another person, a fortiori he may not escape by falsely attributing to others the ideas to which he gives expression.

Here is the third headnote of an opinion from a West reporter. It summarizes a portion of the opinion. (If you went to the body of the opinion, you would find the text which this headnote summarizes preceded by the same number in brackets—here 3.) West also assigns this headnote a key topic and number: Libel and Slander 28. The paragraph will go into the digests of West where the researcher will be able to find other case law under this same topic and number.

HORNBOOK

A hornbook is a treatise (see this entry) on a topic of law written by private individuals. It tries to cover the topic from A to Z with summaries of and commentaries on the law. Hornbooks are different from formbooks (see this entry) in that they are less practice oriented than the latter.

 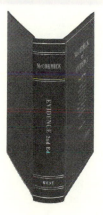

INTERSTATE COMPACT

An interstate compact is an agreement between two or more states governing a problem of mutual concern, e.g., the supervision of the parolee in one state who has moved to another state. The compact is passed by the legislature of each state and is therefore part of the state statutes.

KARDEX

Kardex is a file on which the library records incoming publications that are part of serial or on-going subscriptions. It records the latest volume numbers of reporters received in the mail, the most recent Shepard's pamphlets received, etc. If you were not sure whether certain volumes on the shelf have the latest pocket parts in them, for example, you would ask library staff to check the KARDEX for the most recent material received by the library for those volumes. Not all libraries use Kardex. If a library does not have Kardex files, it has some equivalent system of recording updating material.

LEGAL DICTIONARY

A legal dictionary contains the definitions of words and phrases commonly used in the law.   Commonly used single-volume dictionaries are Black's Law Dictionary (West) and Ballentine's Law Dictionary (Lawyers Co-operative Publishing Co.).   The major multi-volume legal dictionary is Words and Phrases by West.   The definitions consist of thousands of excerpts from court opinions that have treated the word or phrase.   Hence, this set of volumes can serve as an excellent case finder.

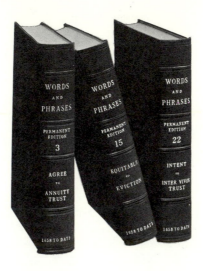

LEGAL ENCYCLOPEDIA

A legal encyclopedia is a multi-volume discussion/summary of almost every legal topic.   They are valuable (a) as background reading in a research topic that is new to you and (b) as case finders due to their extensive footnotes. The two competing national encyclopedias are American Jurisprudence 2d (see this entry) published by Lawyers Co-operative Company, and Corpus Juris Secundum (see this entry) published by West.   A number of states have their own encyclopedias covering the law of that state, e.g., Florida Jurisprudence, Michigan Law and Practice.

LEGAL NEWSPAPER

A legal newspaper is a local daily newspaper published by a private company which lists the court calendars, legal announcements, the full text of some opinions, job announcements, etc.   Most large cities have their own legal newspaper.   It may be called the daily law journal, the daily law reporter, etc.   (See illustration on page 37.)

LEGISLATION

Legislation is the process of making statutory law by the legislature.   It also refers to the statutes themselves.   (See Acts, Acts and Resolves;   Statutory Code)

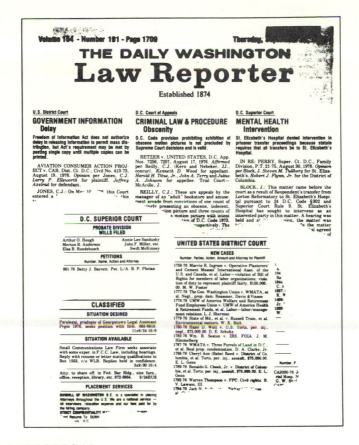

LEGAL PERIODICAL

A legal periodical is a collection of literature in periodicals or pamphlets on specific topics of law.   The periodical is first published as small pamphlets which are later bound by most libraries.   Many legal periodicals are published by law students of law schools and are often called law reviews or law journals. A smaller number of periodicals are published by private companies and by bar associations.

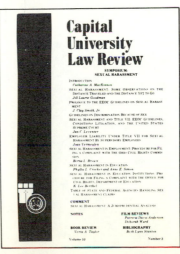

As we shall see later, the major indexes to legal periodical literature are:[12]

- Index to Legal Periodicals
- Current Law Index
- Legal Resource Index

LEXIS

A legal research computer.   (See infra p. 112)

LOOSE LEAF SERVICE

Most law books come in one of three forms:

- pamphlets
- bound volumes
- loose leaf

A loose-leaf text is a three-ring binder containing pages that can easily be put in or taken out.   As new material is written covering the subject-matter of the loose-leaf text, it is placed in the binder, often replacing the pages which the new material has changed or otherwise supplemented.

There are few areas of the law that are *not* covered by one or more loose leaf services.   Examples include: Employment and Safety and Health Guide, Standard Federal Tax Reporter, United States Law Week, Criminal Law Reporter, Family Law Reporter, Media Law Reporter, Sexual Law Reporter, Environmental Law Reporter, Labor Relations Reporter, etc.   Among their features are:

- the full text and/or summaries of court opinions in the area of the specialty
- the full text and/or summaries of administrative regulations and decisions in the area of the specialty (some of which may not be available elsewhere)
- summaries of the major statutory provisions of the specialty
- practical tips on how to practice in the specialty

The major publishers of loose leaf services are Commerce Clearing House (CCH), Bureau of National Affairs (BNA) and Prentice Hall (PH).[13]   Examples:

MARTINDALE-HUBBELL LAW DIRECTORY

A multi-volume set of books that serves three major functions:

- gives an alphabetical listing of attorneys and law firms by state and city
- gives short summaries of the law of all 50 states (see its separate Digest volume)
- gives short summaries of the law of many foreign countries[14] (see its separate Digest volume)

MILITARY JUSTICE REPORTER (M.J.)

See Cases.

MODERN FEDERAL PRACTICE DIGEST

See Digests.

NEW YORK SUPPLEMENT 2d (N.Y.S.2d)

See Cases.

NORTH EASTERN REPORTER 2d (N.E.2d)

See Cases.

NORTH WESTERN DIGEST

See Digests.

NORTH WESTERN REPORTER 2d (N.W.2d)

See Cases.

PACIFIC DIGEST

See Digests.

PACIFIC REPORTER 2d (P.2d)

See Cases.

PRACTICE MANUAL

A formbook (see this entry).

RECORD

The record is the official collection of what happened during a particular trial.   It includes a word-for-word transcript of what was said, the pleadings, exhibits, etc.   (See also Congressional Record.)

REGIONAL DIGEST

See Digests.

RESTATEMENTS

Restatements are scholarly treatises (see this entry) published by the American Law Institute (ALI) which attempt to formulate (i.e., restate) the existing law of a given area.   For example:

Restatement of Agency	Restatement of Judgments
Restatement of Conflicts of Law	Restatement of Property
Restatement of Contracts	Restatement of Security
Restatement of Foreign Relations Law	Restatement of Torts
	Restatement of Trusts

While the restatements are not law since they are written by a private organization (ALI), they are extensively relied upon by courts and cited in their opinions.

RULES OF COURT

Rules of court are usually found in separate rules volumes and/or within the statutory code for the jurisdiction. There are "Desk Copy" sets of rules for the state and federal courts in most states.

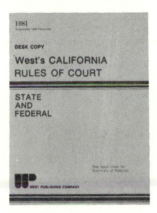

SERIES

Series refers to a new numbering order for new volumes within the *same* set of books. (It should not be confused with edition which refers to a revision of the same book or set of books.) Reporters, for example, come in series. Federal Reporter, First Series (abbreviated "F.") has 300 volumes. After the last volume was printed, the publisher decided to start a new series of the same set of books—Federal Reporter, Second Series (abbreviated "F.2d"). The first volume of F.2d is volume 1. After a large number of F.2d volumes are printed, we will probably see an F.3d which will begin again with volume 1. There is no consistent number of volumes that a publisher will print before it decides to start a new series for a given set of books.

SESSION LAW

See Acts, Acts and Resolves

SHEPARD'S

Our goals in this section are to define what is meant by Shepard's and shepardizing and to identify the major sets of Shepard's volumes that exist. Later in the Chapter we will learn how to use Shepard's—how to shepardize.[15]

    Shepard's Citations are citators (see this entry). To "shepardize" an item means to use the volumes of Shepard's to collect the research references provided for that item. The references differ depending on what you are shepardizing. If, for example, you are shepardizing a case, you will be given the parallel cite for this case (if any); the history of the case, e.g., appeals within the same litigation;   other cases that have mentioned the case you are shepardizing;   legal periodical literature;   and annotations on the case, etc.[16] If you are shepardizing a statute, you will be given the parallel cite for the statute (if any), amendments, repeals or additions to the statute, court opinions that have interpreted the statute, legal periodical literature on the statute, etc.[17]

	– 327 –	ς
	ICT§2.16	622F2d³ı.
₄n89		492FS³774
	– 365 –	
– 946 –	Cir. 4	– 485
Cir. 9	623F2d¹²891	W V:
₂3F2d⁴561	Cir. 5	268Sℤℤ3₍
	623F2d¹⁰359	
– 953 –	623F2d¹¹359	– 5ℱ
Cir. 4	623F2d¹²359	C
₍24F2d³510	623F2d¹³359	613P2
	623F2d¹⁴359	
– 995 –	623F2d¹⁵359	– ℓ
Cir. 7	623F2d¹⁶359	ℂ
491FS⁴970	f623F2d³360	4BR
e491FS¹²972	f623F2d⁷360	
	623F2d¹⁰397	
– 1010 –	623F2d¹¹397	
DC	j623F2d403	492ı
412A2d35	f623F2d	
	[¹⁰1088	
3 – 1202 –	f623F2d	
Cir. 2	[¹²1089	⁄
d490FS⁹1218	f624F2d¹³539	
	f624F2d¹⁰554	
242 – 1209 –	f624F2d¹¹55₄	
Kan	f624F2d¹²5ℭ	
′– 615P2d135	f624F2d¹ⁿ	
₅	f624F2⁻	

What can you shepardize?   A partial list is as follows:

- Court opinions
- Statutes
- Constitutions
- Some administrative regulations
- Some administrative decisions
- Ordinances
- Charters
- Rules of Court
- Some executive orders
- Some treaties
- Restatements
- Legal periodical literature

The following is an overview of some of these items that can be shepardized with the sets of Shepard's used:

You want to shepardize an opinion of the United States Supreme Court:

Here is the set of Shepard's you use to shepardize an opinion of the United States Supreme Court:

Supreme Court Reporter, *or* United States Supreme Court Reports (L.Ed.) *or* United States Reports.

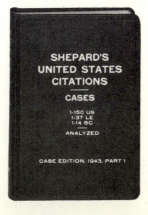

Shepard's United States Citations, Case Edition

You want to shepardize opinions found in Federal Reporter, 2d:

Federal Reporter, 2d

Here is the set of Shepard's you use to shepardize a F.Supp. opinion:

Shepard's Federal Citations

You want to shepardize opinions found in Federal Supplement:

Federal Supplement

Here is the set of Shepard's you use to shepardize an opinion of the United States Supreme Court:

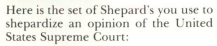

Shepard's Federal Citations

You want to shepardize a statute of Congress or a statute found in USCA (United States Code Annotated) or in USCS (United States Code Service) or in USC (United States Code):

Here is the set of Shepard's that you use to shepardize a federal statute:

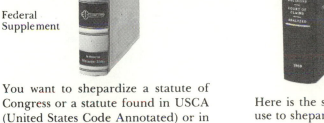

Shepard's United States Citations, Statute Edition.

The same set of Shepard's (United States Citations, Statute Edition) can be used to shepardize:
A U.S. constitutional provision
A U.S. treaty
A rule of court of the federal courts

You want to shepardize a regulation of a federal agency found in CFR:

Regulation in CFR

Here is the set of Shepard's that will enable you to shepardize a regulation in CFR:

Shepard's Code of Federal Regulations Citations

You want to shepardize opinions found within the following regional reporters:

Atlantic Reporter 2d
Pacific Reporter 2d
South Western Reporter 2d
South Eastern Reporter 2d
North Eastern Reporter 2d

Other regional reporters:
North Western Reporter 2d
Southern Reporter 2d

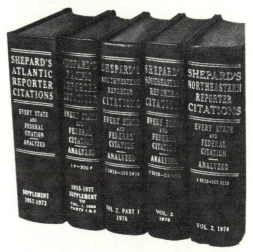

Here are the sets of Shepard's that you use to shepardize the opinions in these regional reporters

You want to shepardize the following:

A Rhode Island court opinion
A Rhode Island statute
A Rhode Island constitutional provision
A New Hampshire court opinion
A New Hampshire statute
A New Hampshire constitutional provision

Here are the sets of Shepard's that you would use.

Every state has its own set of Shepard's similar to Shepard's Rhode Island Citations and Shepard's New Hampshire Citations above.

Other sets of Shepard's include:

Shepard's United States Administrative Citations
> (enabling you to shepardize the administrative decisions of some federal agencies)

Shepard's United States Patents and Trademarks Citations
> (enabling you to shepardize patents, trademarks and copyrights)

Shepard's Federal Labor Law Citations
> (enabling you to shepardize administrative decisions of the National Labor Relations Board)

Shepard's Law Review Citations
> (enabling you to shepardize legal periodical literature that has been cited in court opinions)

Shepard's Restatements of the Law Citations
> (enabling you to shepardize restatements of ALI that have been cited in court opinions)

Shepard's Military Justice Citations
> (enabling you to shepardize decisions and rules relating to military law)

Shepard's Criminal Justice Citations
> (enabling you to shepardize the American Bar Association's Standards Relating to the Administration of Criminal Justice)

Shepard's Acts and Cases by Popular Name
> (enabling you to shepardize cases and statutes through their popular name)

Shepard's Code of Professional Responsibility Citations
> (enabling you to shepardize the American Bar Association's code of conduct for lawyers and judges)

Shepard's Bankruptcy Citations
> (enabling you to shepardize administrative and court material on bankruptcy)

SLIP LAW

A slip law is the form in which laws or acts of Legislatures are first printed. They may be printed on several pieces of paper or in pamphlet forms depending upon the length of the act.

Public Law 87-17
87th Congress, H. R. 4363
April 7, 1961

AN ACT

75 STAT. 41.

To amend Public Law 86-272 relating to State taxation of interstate commerce.

Be it enacted by the Senate and House of Representatives of the United States of America in Congress assembled, That section 201 of Public Law 86-272 (73 Stat. 556) is amended to read as follows:

"SEC. 201. The Committee on the Judiciary of the House of Representatives and the Committee on Finance of the United States Senate, acting separately or jointly, or both, or any duly authorized subcommittees thereof, shall make full and complete studies of all matters pertaining to the taxation of interstate commerce by the States, territories, and possessions of the United States, the District of Columbia, and the Commonwealth of Puerto Rico, or any political or taxing subdivision of the foregoing."

Interstate commerce.
Taxation studies.
15 USC 381 note.

Approved April 7, 1961.

Most slip laws are later printed in volumes called Session Laws, Acts, Statutes at Large, (see Acts, Acts and Resolves) and finally are printed in statutory codes (see this entry).

SLIP OPINION

When a court first announces a decision it is usually published in what is called a slip opinion or slip decision. It contains a single case in pamphlet form. The slip opinions are later printed in advance sheets (see this entry) which in turn become bound reporters (see case).

SOUTH EASTERN DIGEST

See Digests.

SOUTH EASTERN REPORTER 2d (S.E.2d)

See Cases.

SOUTHERN DIGEST

See Digests.

SOUTHERN REPORTER 2d (S.2d)

See Cases.

SOUTH WESTERN REPORTER 2d (S.W.2d)

See Cases.

STATUTES AT LARGE

See Acts, Acts and Resolves. *See also* United States Statutes at Large

STATUTORY CODE

A statutory code is a collection of the statutes of the legislature organized by subject matter, e.g., the statutes on murder are in one place, the statutes on probate are together. Statutory codes are usually also annotated, meaning that there are research references provided along with the full text of the statute, e.g., summaries of cases that have interpreted the statute, information on the legislative history of the statute such as amendments.

Example of a state statutory code

The three major codes of federal statutes of Congress:

USCA—United States Code Annotated (published by West)
USCS—United States Code Service (published by Lawyers Co-operative Publishing Company)
USC—United States Code (published by the U.S. Government)

SUPREME COURT REPORTER (S.Ct.)

See Cases.

TOTAL CLIENT-SERVICE LIBRARY

The Total Client Service Library is the system by which Lawyer's Co-operative Publishing Company refers you to many of the law books it publishes.   If, for example, you are reading an annotation in ALR, or ALR2d, or ALR3d or ALR4th or ALR Fed (see this entry), you will be referred to other Lawyers Co-op books on the same subject matter, e.g., American Jurisprudence 2d, USCS (United States Code Service), Federal Procedural Forms L.Ed., Am Jur Pleading and Practice Forms, etc.

TOTAL CLIENT-SERVICE LIBRARY® REFERENCES

62 Am Jur 2d, Process §§ 100, 102

1 Federal Procedural Forms I. Ed, Actions in District Court § 1:745

11 Am Jur Pl & Pr Forms (Rev Ed), Federal Practice and Procedure,
   Form 292; 20 Am Jur Pl & Pr Forms (Rev Ed), Process, Forms 142,
   143

USCS, Court Rules, Rules of Civil Procedure for United States District
   Courts, Rule 4(d)(1)

US L Ed Digest, Writ and Process § 24

ALR Digests, Writ and Process §§ 12, 20, 22, 23

L Ed Index to Annos, Age; Discretion; Writ and Process

ALR Quick Index, Age; Constructive or Substituted Service of Process;
   Discretion; Rules of Civil Procedure

Federal Quick Index, Age; Constructive or Substituted Service of Process; Discretion; Federal Rules of Civil Procedure

TREATISE

A treatise (not to be confused with treaty) is any book written by private individuals on a topic of law. They try to give an extensive treatment of that topic. Hornbooks (see this entry) and formbooks (see this entry) are also considered treatises.

UNITED STATES CODE (USC)

See Statutory Code.

UNITED STATES CODE ANNOTATED (USCA)

See Statutory Code.

U.S. CODE CONGRESSIONAL AND ADMINISTRATIVE NEWS (U.S.C.C.A.N.)

This set of books published by West will enable you to:

- Obtain leads to the legislative history of federal statutes (primarily through its Table 4)
- Obtain the complete text of public laws of Congress
- Obtain the complete text of some Congressional committee reports (important for legislative history)
- Translate a Statute at Large cite into a USC/USCA/USCS cite (through Table 2)
- Obtain the complete text of some federal agency regulations (duplicating some of what is found in the Code of Federal Regulations—C.F.R.)
- Obtain the complete text of executive orders and other executive documents
- Obtain the complete text of all current United States Statutes at Large (see this entry)

Table 4
LEGISLATIVE HISTORY

Bill numbers in parentheses ( ) are companion bills reported either in the Senate or the House

Public Law				Report No. 91–		Comm. Reporting		Cong.Rec.Vol. 116 (1970) Dates of Consideration and Passage	
No.91–	Date App.	84 Stat. Page	Bill No.	House	Senate	House	Senate	House	Ser
191	Feb. 3	3	S.J.Res. 181	810	133	PA	FR	Jan. 30	N
192	Feb. 4	4	H.J.Res.	none	647	none	J	Jan. 38	
193				ne		none	none	Feb. 7	
						App	App	De	
							J		
							Agr'		

UNITED STATES CODE SERVICE (USCS)

See Statutory Code.

UNITED STATES LAW WEEK (U.S.L.W.)

See Cases.

OUTLINE OF LEGAL REFERENCE MATERIALS

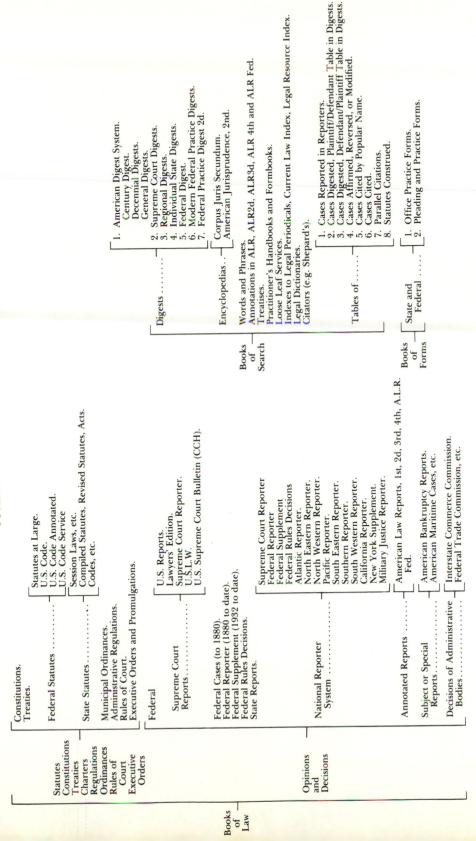

Books of Law

Statutes
Constitutions
Treaties
Charters
Regulations
Ordinances
Rules of Court
Executive Orders

- Constitutions.
- Treaties.

Federal Statutes ....
- Statutes at Large.
- U.S. Code.
- U.S. Code Annotated.
- U.S. Code Service

State Statutes ....
- Session Laws, etc.
- Compiled Statutes, Revised Statutes, Acts.
- Codes, etc.

- Municipal Ordinances.
- Administrative Regulations.
- Rules of Court.
- Executive Orders and Promulgations.

Opinions and Decisions

Federal
- U.S. Reports.
- Lawyers' Edition.

Supreme Court Reports ....
- Supreme Court Reporter.
- U.S.L.W.
- U.S. Supreme Court Bulletin (CCH).

- Federal Cases (to 1880).
- Federal Reporter (1880 to date).
- Federal Supplement (1932 to date).
- Federal Rules Decisions.
- State Reports.

National Reporter System ....
- Supreme Court Reporter
- Federal Reporter
- Federal Supplement
- Federal Rules Decisions
- Atlantic Reporter.
- North Eastern Reporter.
- North Western Reporter.
- Pacific Reporter.
- South Eastern Reporter.
- Southern Reporter.
- South Western Reporter.
- California Reporter.
- New York Supplement.
- Military Justice Reporter.

Annotated Reports ....
- American Law Reports, 1st, 2d, 3rd, 4th, A.L.R. Fed.

Subject or Special Reports ....
- American Bankruptcy Reports.
- American Maritime Cases, etc.

Decisions of Administrative Bodies ....
- Interstate Commerce Commission.
- Federal Trade Commission, etc.

Books of Search

Digests ....
1. American Digest System.
   - Century Digest.
   - Decennial Digests.
   - General Digests.
2. Supreme Court Digests.
3. Regional Digests.
4. Individual State Digests.
5. Federal Digest.
6. Modern Federal Practice Digests.
7. Federal Practice Digest 2d.

Encyclopedias ....
- Corpus Juris Secundum.
- American Jurisprudence, 2nd.

- Words and Phrases.
- Annotations in ALR, ALR2d, ALR3d, ALR 4th and ALR Fed.
- Treatises.
- Practitioner's Handbooks and Formbooks.
- Loose Leaf Services.
- Indexes to Legal Periodicals, Current Law Index, Legal Resource Index.
- Legal Dictionaries.
- Citators (e.g. Shepard's).

Tables of ....
1. Cases Reported in Reporters.
2. Cases Digested, Plaintiff/Defendant Table in Digests.
3. Cases Digested, Defendant/Plaintiff Table in Digests.
4. Cases Affirmed, Reversed, or Modified.
5. Cases Cited by Popular Name.
6. Cases Cited.
7. Parallel Citations.
8. Statutes Construed.

Books of Forms

State and Federal ....
1. Office Practice Forms.
2. Pleading and Practice Forms.

UNITED STATES REPORTS (U.S.)

See Cases.

UNITED STATES STATUTES AT LARGE

The United States Statutes at Large (abbreviated "Stat.") contains the full text of every public law and private law of Congress.   The set is official since it is published by the government.   The statutes within it are printed chronologically.   (The public laws are later codified and printed in one of the three sets of codified federal statutes: USC, USCA, USCS) (see Statutory Code). All current statutes at large are now printed in U.S. Code Congressional and Administrative News (see this entry) as well as in separate Stat. volumes.

UNITED STATES SUPREME COURT BULLETIN (CCH)

See Cases.

UNITED STATES SUPREME COURT DIGEST L.Ed.

See Digests.

UNITED STATES SUPREME COURT DIGEST (WEST)

See Digests.

UNITED STATES SUPREME COURT REPORTS, L.Ed.

See Cases.

WESTLAW

A legal research computer.   (See infra p. 112)

Section I.   LEGAL AUTHORITY

The objective of legal research is to find authority that applies to the facts of the client's case.   First some basic definitions:

- Authority: Whatever a court could rely on in reaching a decision.
- Primary Authority or source: Any *law* that a court could rely on in reaching a decision (e.g., statute, opinion, constitution, administrative decision and regulation, ordinance, charter, executive order, rule of court, treaty).
- Secondary Authority or source: Any *non-law* that a court could rely on in reaching a decision (e.g., legal periodical literature, practice manual, treatise, legal encyclopedia, annotation).
- Mandatory Authority: Any primary authority that a court *must* rely on in reaching a decision.
- Persuasive Authority: Any non-mandatory primary authority and any secondary authority which a court feels is convincing enough (i.e., persuasive enough) to give it some guidance in reaching a decision (a court is not required to accept persuasive authority).

- Non-Authority: Non-authority has three meanings:
  - (a) Digests, Shepard's, indexes, etc. which are used only to find authority and are never relied on as authority themselves.
  - (b) Any primary or secondary authority that is not "on point", i.e., it does not cover the facts of the problem you are researching.
  - (c) Any primary authority that does not validly extend into the geographic boundary (i.e., geographic jurisdiction) of the court where you are in litigation (called the forum court).

There is never any dispute as to whether something is primary or secondary authority. Only primary authority consists of laws. It is also clear that secondary authority can *never* be mandatory, e.g., a court never is required to follow what a law review article says, nor what a treatise such as a restatement says. The more complicated questions are:

- When is primary authority considered mandatory authority so that a court must rely on it in reaching its decision?
- When is primary authority considered persuasive authority so that a court is free to accept or reject it in reaching its decision?
- When is primary authority considered non-authority?

Let us assume that you have litigation underway or pending in a particular court. We will call this the *forum* court. (Forum simply means the place where the litigation is brought.) As the chart on page 52 shows, there is a large variety of primary authority on which you could potentially ask the forum court to rely.

Review the three definitions of non-authority presented above. We are not concerned with definition (a) since none of the items in the middle column of the chart are digests, Shepard's etc. Such items are always non-authority. Definition (b) refers to primary or secondary authority. Nothing in the middle column is secondary authority since everything there is a law—everything is primary authority. Definition (b) tells us that all primary authority is non-authority if it is not "on point." The same is true for any secondary authority.

What is meant by "on point"? It means "covering the facts of the research problem." More specifically:

- Secondary authority is on point if the discussion in the treatise, encyclopedia, law review article, etc. covers the facts of the research problem. If it does, it can be persuasive authority, but can never be mandatory authority, as we have seen. If it does not, then the secondary authority is non-authority.
- A statute is on point if the intent of the legislature was to have the statute cover the facts of the research problem. If not, then the statute is non-authority.
- A constitutional provision is on point if the intent of the authors of the constitution was to have the provision cover the facts of the problem. If not, the provision is non-authority.
- A charter, ordinance, administrative regulation, executive order, or treaty is on point if the intent of their authors was to cover the facts of the research problem. If not, they are non-authority.
- A court opinion is on point if the key facts of the opinion are *analogous*[18]

THE MANDATORY/PERSUASIVE/NON-AUTHORITY QUESTIONS		
LAWS WHICH YOU TRY TO ASK A COURT TO RELY ON:		
THE FORUM: The place where the court sits before which you have litigation in process or pending.	—The federal (U.S.) constitution —The state constitution of the forum —The state constitution of one of the other 49 states —The charter of the forum —A non-forum charter —A federal statute of Congress —A state statute of the forum —A state statute of one of the other 49 states —An ordinance of the forum —A non-forum ordinance —A federal court opinion —A state court opinion of the forum —A state court opinion of one of the other 49 states —A federal administrative regulation —A state administrative regulation of the forum —A state administrative regulation of one of the other 49 states —A federal administrative decision —A state administrative decision of the forum —A state administrative decision of one of the other 49 states —A rule of court of a federal court —A rule of court of a state court of the forum —A rule of court of a state court of one of the other 49 states —An executive order of the U.S. President —An executive order of a foreign country —An executive order of the governor of the forum —An executive order of the governor of one of the other 49 states —A U.S. treaty —A non-U.S. treaty	When are these laws mandatory authority? When are they only persuasive authority? When are they non-authority?

(i.e., sufficiently similar) to the facts of the research problem.
• An administrative decision is on point if the key facts of the decision are analogous to the facts of the research problem.

In short, to determine whether any law (primary authority) is on point you must go through *legal analysis* of the law.[19]

GENERAL PRINCIPLES OF MANDATORY AUTHORITY, PERSUASIVE AUTHORITY, AND NON-AUTHORITY

1. A provision of the U.S. Constitution that is on point is mandatory authority on all state and federal forum courts.

2. A statute of Congress that is on point is mandatory authority on all state and federal forum courts.   The statute of Congress must be authorized by the U.S. Constitution.   Otherwise, it is invalid and non-authority in any forum.

3. A federal administrative regulation or decision that is on point is mandatory authority on all state and federal forum courts.   The regulation or decision must be authorized by the U.S. Constitution and/or a statute of Congress.   Otherwise, it is invalid and non-authority in any forum.

4. A federal treaty or executive order that is on point is mandatory authority on all state and federal forum courts.   The treaty or order must be authorized by the U.S. Constitution and/or a statute of Congress.   Otherwise, it is invalid and non-authority.

5. An on-point opinion of the United States Supreme Court interpreting a provision of the U.S. Constitution, a statute of Congress, an administrative regulation or decision of a federal agency, an executive order or treaty is mandatory authority on all state and federal forum courts.

6. An on-point opinion of any of the eleven United States Courts of Appeal interpreting any of the laws listed in #5 above is mandatory authority on all state and federal forum courts within the geographic boundary or jurisdiction of that U.S. Court of appeal.   It is persuasive authority outside that boundary or jurisdiction.

7. An on-point opinion of a United States District Court interpreting any of the laws listed in #5 above is mandatory authority on all state and federal courts within the geographic boundary or jurisdiction of that U.S. District Court.   It is persuasive authority outside that boundary or jurisdiction.

8. A provision of a state constitution that is on point is mandatory authority only within that state.   It is not persuasive authority in other states.   It is non-authority in other states.   (For exceptions, see #13 and #14 below.) The state constitution cannot conflict with the U.S. Constitution, a valid federal statute, a valid federal regulation, etc.   If there is conflict, the state constitution is invalid and non-authority.

9. A state statute that is on point is mandatory authority only within that state.   It is not persuasive authority in other states.   It is non-authority in other states.   (For exceptions, see #13 and #14 below.)   The state statute must not conflict with any valid federal law.   If it is in conflict, the state statute is invalid and non-authority.

10. A state administrative regulation, or state executive order that is on point is mandatory authority only within that state.   It is not persuasive authority in other states.   It is non-authority in other states.   (For exceptions, see #13 and #14 below.)   If it conflicts with valid federal law, it is invalid and non-authority.

11. An on-point opinion of the highest state court interpreting its own state law is mandatory authority on all lower state forum courts in that state.   It can be persuasive authority outside the state.   The geographic boundary or jurisdiction of this court is the state itself.   The opinion must not conflict with valid federal law.   If it does, it is invalid and non-authority.

12. An on-point opinion of a middle appeals state court interpreting its own state law is mandatory on all lower forum state courts within the geographic boundary or jurisdiction of that middle appeals court.   It can be persuasive

outside that boundary or jurisdiction. The opinion must not conflict with valid federal law. If it does, it is invalid and non-authority.

13. The conflict-of-law rules of a state may sometimes require it to apply the laws of another state (e.g., when the events of an accident or of a breach of contract occur in more than one state). In such cases, a forum court of one state will apply a statute, opinion or constitutional provision of another state.

14. The full-faith-and-credit clause of the U.S. Constitution sometimes requires one state to recognize and apply the laws of another state (e.g., a valid divorce in one state must be recognized as valid in the forum state). In such cases, a forum court of one state must apply a statute, opinion or constitutional provision of another state.

15. A rule of court that is on point is mandatory authority only for practice before that court whether it is a state or federal forum court.

16. A charter or ordinance that is on point is mandatory authority within the geographic boundary or jurisdiction in the municipality or county. It is non-authority elsewhere. If it conflicts with valid state or federal law, it is invalid and non-authority.

17. When common law (i.e., judge-made law) conflicts with a statute in the same state, the statute controls. Statutes are superior in authority to common law. When in conflict, the mandatory authority is the statute.

18. Dictum is never mandatory authority. It is persuasive authority. Dictum is anything a court says in an opinion that is not necessary to the holding of the opinion.[20]

Example: The forum court where you are in litigation is a New York state trial court. The case involves a property ownership dispute between two New York residents. The property is in New York.

Examples of mandatory authority for this trial court:

- New York state statutes that are on point
- New York state constitutional provisions that are on point
- Opinions of the highest state court in New York that are on point
- Opinions of the middle appeals court in New York whose geographic boundary or jurisdiction includes the forum trial court (the opinions, of course, must be on point)
- State administrative regulations or decisions that are on point
- Charters or ordinances that are on point
- Rules of court of the forum trial court that are on point

Examples of persuasive authority for this trial court:

- The opinion of any state court within the other 49 states
- An opinion of a middle appeals court in New York whose geographic boundary or jurisdiction does not include the forum trial court
- Dictum in any opinion
- A restatement that is on point (e.g., a section of the Restatement of Property[21])
- Any other treatise that is on point
- A law review article that is on point
- A section in a legal encyclopedia that is on point

- Anything in a legal dictionary that is on point
- An annotation in ALR, ALR2d, ALR3d, ALR4th or ALR Fed

Non-authority for this trial court:

- Anything in a digest, Shepard's, an index, etc.
- Any law (primary authority) that is not on point
- Any secondary authority that is not on point
- Any invalid law
- Statutes, regulations, ordinances, charters, rules of court, etc. of any of the other 49 states (unless conflict-of-law or full-faith-and-credit principles apply)

One final problem remains to be considered.   When is a state court opinion mandatory on a federal forum court?   The following principle applies:

> *Whenever the highest state court is interpreting the state constitution or a state statute, the interpretation is mandatory on every federal court.   The federal court must accept the meaning given the state constitution or statute by this state court. If, for example, a state court says that a state statute requiring "periodic TB examinations" means an exam every three years, a federal court cannot say that it means every ten years.   Having accepted the state court's interpretation, the federal court can then ask whether the state statute so interpreted is in violation of the U.S. Constitution or a U.S. statute.   This is a separate issue from the meaning of a state constitution or statute.*

Section J.   CITATION FORM

A citation or cite is a reference to any written material.   The cite tells you where you can go in the library to find the cited material.

The first question we must face is: are there any consistent rules on citation form?   If you pick up different law books and examine the citations of similar material within them, you will notice a great variety of citation form. You will find that people abbreviate things differently, they do not include the same order of information in the cite, they use parentheses differently, they use punctuation within the cite differently, they include different amounts of information in the cite, etc.   There does not appear to be any consistency.   Yet, in spite of this diversity and confusion, you are often scolded by supervisors for failing to use "proper citation form."   What, you may well ask, is "proper"?

Start by checking the rules of court [22] of the court that will have jurisdiction over the problem you are researching.   There may or may not be citation rules within it.   If such rules exist, they must obviously be followed in spite of what any other citation rule book may say.   These are, in effect, citation *laws*.   The following is an excerpt Michigan rules of court that *do* contain citation rules:

In the Matter of Michigan Uniform System of Citations

On Order of the Court, all courts within the State of Michigan and all reported decisions of this Court and the Michigan Court of Appeals shall adhere to and follow the

---

CITATION FORM—continued

CITATION FORM—continued

"Michigan Uniform System of Citations" set forth in the pages attached hereto and made a part hereof, to be effective February 1, 1972.

Statutes.

1. Michigan statutes.

   (a) Do *not* use the section symbol "§" or "sec." or "section" in citing Compiled Laws, MCLA and MSA

   (b) Public acts: cite year, "PA", and act number, *e.g.,* 1945 PA 87

   (c) Compiled Laws of 1948: cite as 1948 CL

   (d) Michigan Compiled Laws Annotated: cite as MCLA (Do *not* indicate a Cumulative Supplement.)

   (e) Michigan Statutes Annotated: cite as MSA
   (Do *not* use the date of a revised volume or indicate a Cumulative Supplement.)

   (f) If the original public act used Roman numerals for sections or parts of the act, use these Roman numerals rather than Arabic numerals.

   (g) Parallel citations should include MSA. They should be separated by semicolons and *not* placed in parentheses.

   Examples: MCLA 600.407; MSA 27A.407
   1931 PA 328, § 360, as amended by 1947 PA 190; 1948 CL (or MCLA) 750.360; MSA 28.592.

Suppose, however, that there are no official citation rules in the rules of court for your court, or that these citation rules do not cover the citation question that you have. In such circumstances, *ask your supervisor what citation form you should use.* You will probably be told to "use the Blue Book." This is a reference to the Uniform System of Citation which we looked at earlier.[23] It is a small blue pamphlet (although in earlier editions, white covers were used). The Blue Book is published by a group of law students on the law reviews [24] of their law schools. Caution is needed, however, in using the Blue Book. It is a highly technical and sometimes difficult-to-use pamphlet because it packs so much information in a relatively small space. The main audience of the Blue Book is the law reviews of the law schools who send their manuscripts to a professional printer for type setting. There are directions in the Blue Book, for example, on the type size for certain kinds of lettering. Such directions would not apply to the normal kind of memorandum of law which is the product of most research assignments. Also, be aware of the fact that many courts do *not* follow the Blue Book even if there are no rules of court on citation form for that court. Judges often simply use their own system of citation without necessarily being consistent in the citation forms used.

GUIDELINES ON CITATION FORM

1. Find out if there are citation rules in the rules of court.
2. Ask your supervisor if s/he has any special instructions on citation form.
3. Consult the Blue Book.
4. Consult the basic citation rules presented below.
5. Remember that the purpose of a citation is to enable a reader of your writing to be able to locate in a library what you are citing. This is the functional purpose of a citation. You must give enough information in the cite to fulfill this purpose. Courtesy to the reader is as important as compliance with the niceties of citation form.

GUIDELINES—continued

GUIDELINES—continued

> 6. Often a private publisher of a book will tell you how to cite the book. ("Cite this book as . . . ") Ignore this instruction! Instead, follow guidelines 1–5 above.
> 7. When in doubt about whether to include something in a citation after carefully following guidelines 1–5 above, resolve the doubt by including it in the cite.

BASIC CITATION RULES

Use the following citation forms [25] unless instructions 1–3 in the above chart tell you otherwise:

I. Citing Opinions

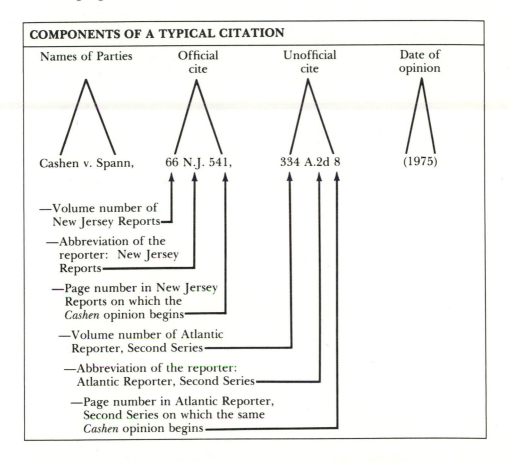

COMPONENTS OF A TYPICAL CITATION

Names of Parties   Official cite   Unofficial cite   Date of opinion

Cashen v. Spann,   66 N.J. 541,   334 A.2d 8   (1975)

—Volume number of New Jersey Reports

—Abbreviation of the reporter: New Jersey Reports

—Page number in New Jersey Reports on which the *Cashen* opinion begins

—Volume number of Atlantic Reporter, Second Series

—Abbreviation of the reporter: Atlantic Reporter, Second Series

—Page number in Atlantic Reporter, Second Series on which the same *Cashen* opinion begins

The following are the most common kinds of opinions and decisions that you will be citing:

EXAMPLE A: FORMAT OF A CITATION TO AN OPINION OF THE HIGHEST FEDERAL COURT (the United States Supreme Court):

Taglianetti v. United States, 394 U.S. 316, 89 S.Ct. 1099, 22 L.Ed.2d 302 (1969)

EXAMPLE B: FORMAT OF A CITATION TO AN OPINION OF A FEDERAL MIDDLE APPEALS COURT (the United States Court of Appeals, Second Circuit):

> *Sterling Nat'l Bank and Trust Co. of N. Y. v. Fidelity Mortgage Investors,* 510 F.2d 870 (2nd Cir. 1975).

EXAMPLE C: FORMAT OF A CITATION TO AN OPINION OF A FEDERAL TRIAL COURT (the United States District Court, Western District in Wisconsin):

> *Stone v. Schmidt,* 398 F.Supp. 768 (W.D.Wisc.1975)

EXAMPLE D: FORMAT OF A CITATION TO AN OPINION OF THE HIGHEST STATE COURT (New Jersey Supreme Court):

> *Petlin Associates, Inc. v. Township of Dover,* 64 N.J. 327, 316 A.2d 1 (1974)

EXAMPLE E: FORMAT OF A CITATION TO AN OPINION OF A LOWER STATE COURT (Conn. Superior Court, Appellate Session):

> *Huckabee v. Stevens,* 32 Conn.Sup. 511, 338 A.2d 512 (Conn.Super., App.Sess., 1975)

EXAMPLE F: FORMAT OF A CITATION TO AN ADMINISTRATIVE DECISION (National Labor Relations Board):

> *Standard Dry Wall Products, Inc.,* 91 N.L.R.B. 544 (1950)

EXAMPLE G: FORMAT OF A CITATION TO AN OPINION OF THE ATTORNEY GENERAL:

> 40 Op.Atty.Gen. 423 (1945)

Comments:

- A parallel cite to an opinion is another reporter where the exact same opinion (word for word) can be found. Do not confuse (a) a parallel cite (or cites) to an opinion with cites to opinions within the same litigation. As a case goes up on appeal, several opinions may be written at the different court levels. These opinions are part of the history of the case.[26] The opinions are *not* parallel cites to each other.
- Always provide parallel cites that exist. At the time of your research, the parallel cite may not yet exist since one of the reporters that will contain the opinion is not out yet. If so, you can only provide the cite to the reporter that is out. (Some believe that you should not provide parallel cites to opinions of the U.S. Supreme Court. They say that the U.S. (official) cite to U.S. Reports is sufficient. A better view is to include the other parallel cites—the Supreme Court Reporter (S.Ct.) and the Lawyer's Edition (L.Ed.)[27] and the ALR, ALR2d, ALR3d, ALR4th, ALR Fed cite if the latter exists. See Example A on page 57. Everything other than the U.S. cite is an unofficial cite when the reporters are printed by private publishers.[28])

● There are four main techniques to finding a parallel cite:
   1. Shepardize the case.[29]   The first cite in parenthesis in Shepard's is the
      parallel cite.   If you find no cite in parenthesis, it means (a) that no
      parallel cite exists, (b) that the reporter containing the parallel cite has
      not been printed yet, or (c) the parallel cite was given in one of the
      earlier units of Shepard's and not repeated in the unit you are examining.

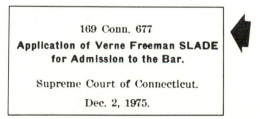

   2. National Reporter Blue Book.[30]   Go to this set of books published by
      West to try to locate a parallel cite.   The National Reporter Blue Book
      will also tell you which official reporters have been discontinued.
   3. Top of the caption.   Go to the reporter[31] that contains the opinion.
      At the beginning of the opinion, there is a caption giving the names of
      the parties, the court, etc.   At the top of this caption, see if there is a
      parallel cite.   (This technique does not often work, but it is worth a try.)
      The following is an excerpt from a caption that does provide a parallel
      cite:

169 Conn. 677

**Application of Verne Freeman SLADE
for Admission to the Bar.**

Supreme Court of Connecticut.

Dec. 2, 1975.

   4. Table of Cases in Digest.   Go to every digest[32] that gives small paragraph
      summaries of court opinions for the court that wrote the opinion, e.g.,
      American Digest System, Federal Practice Digest 2d.   Go to the table
      of cases in these digests.   See if there is a parallel cite for your case.
      In the following excerpt from a digest table of cases you find two cites
      for Ames v. State Bar—106 Cal.Rptr.489 and 506 P.2d 625:

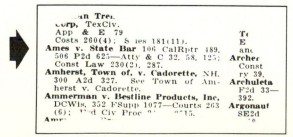

- When parallel cites exist, always place the official cite first before the unofficial cite. (See Examples A, D and E above.)
- There is no parallel cite for Federal Reporter 2d cases (F.2d). (See Example B.) Abbreviate the Circuit in parenthesis at the end of the cite before the year. 2nd Cir. means the opinion was decided by the U.S. Court of Appeals for the Second Circuit. D.C. Cir. would mean the case was decided by the U.S. Court of Appeals for the District of Columbia Circuit. The caption of the opinion will tell you which circuit court wrote the opinion.
- There is no parallel cite for Federal Supplement cases (F. Supp.) (See Example C.) Abbreviate the U.S. District Court in parenthesis at the end of the cite before the year. W.D. Wisc. means the opinion was written by the United States District Court, Western District sitting in Wisconsin. The caption of the opinion will tell you which U.S. District Court wrote the opinion.
- Note the abbreviation N.J. in Example D. Whenever a reporter is abbreviated by the initials of a state, you know that the highest state court in that state wrote the opinion. There is no need, therefore, to abbreviate the name of the court in parenthesis at the end of the cite before the date. N.J. are the initials of the state of New Jersey. Therefore, you know that the highest state court in New Jersey wrote the *Petlin* case in Example D.
- In Example E, none of the reporters are abbreviated by the initials of a state. You must therefore include the abbreviation of the court that wrote the opinion in parenthesis at the end of the cite before the date.
- Include only the last name of individual parties in litigation and do not include their titles, e.g., Commissioner, even if you know such information from the caption of the opinion.
- If multiple party names are given for the plaintiff and defendant in the caption of the opinion, give the last names of the first parties listed on each side.
- Include the date of the decision at the end of the cite in parenthesis. If more than one date is given in the caption of the opinion, include the date the opinion was "decided."
- Do not include the docket number of the case in the cite.

The reporter volumes that contain current opinions are conveniently arranged by volume number. All the volumes of the same set have the same name, e.g., Atlantic Reporter, 2d; New York Reports, etc. There was a time, however, when life was not this simple. Volumes of opinions were identified by the name of the individual person who had responsibility for compiling the opinions written by the judges. These individuals were called reporters. "7 Cush.1" refers to an opinion found on page 1 of volume 7 of Massachusetts cases when Mr. Cushing was the official reporter. When he ended his employment, Mr. Gray took over and the cite of an opinion in the volume immediately after "7 Cush." was "1 Gray 1." Simply by looking at the cover of the volume, you could *not* tell what court's opinions were inside. These volumes are called nominative reporters because they are identified by the name of the individual person who compiled the opinions for the court. If you find such a cite, check a comprehensive abbreviation table (such as the one at the end of every Corpus Juris Secundum volume[33]). There you will learn the full name of this individual reporter and what court's opinions he compiled or reported.

What do you do if you do not have the volume or page of any reporter that has the opinion?   Assume that all you know are the names of the parties and the name of the court that wrote the opinion. How do you obtain the full cite?

1. Go to every digest that covers that reporter.   Check its table of cases.
2. Call the court clerk where the opinion was written.   If it is a recent case, they may be able to send you a copy.   Occasionally, the clerk will give you the cite of the case.   (It may help if you can tell the clerk the docket number of the case.)
3. Go to the reporter volumes that cover the court that wrote the opinion. Since you do not have a volume number, you cannot go directly to the volume that has the opinion.   If, however, you can *approximate* the date of the case, you can check the table of cases in each reporter volume that probably covers that year.   You may have to check the table of cases in 10–15 volumes before achieving success.   The opinions are printed in the reporters in rough chronological order.

When quoting from or referring to specific language in an opinion, you must list both the number of the page on which the opinion begins and the number of the page on which the quoted language begins.   The latter page number is inserted in the citation immediately following the former, and is set off with a comma.

EXAMPLE

"Even though laches may not apply, one must use reasonable promptness when availing himself of judicial protection."   *Bridgeton Education Ass'n. v. Board of Education*, 147 Md. 17, 20, 334 A.2d 376, 379 (1975).

II.   Citing Constitutions and Charters

Constitutions and charters are cited to (a) the abbreviated name of the constitution or charter, (b) the article, and (c) the section to which you are referring.   Where appropriate, you may also cite to the particular clause to which you are referring.

EXAMPLE

"No Bill of Attainder or ex post facto Law shall be passed."   U.S.Const. Art. I, § 9, cl. 3.

In citing constitutions and charters, the date of enactment should *not* be given unless the provision you are citing has been amended or repealed.

III.   Citing Federal Statutes

1. Most federal statutes are collected in chronological order of passage in the *United States Statutes at Large* (Stat.) and subsequently are arranged by subject matter in the *United States Code* (USC).   The general practice is to cite only to the United States Code.   However, in the event that the wording of the

statute differs between the two volumes, you should rely upon and cite to the U.S. Statutes at Large.

2. Statutes in the United States Code are cited to (a) the title number, (b) the abbreviated name of the code, (c) the number of the section and, if relevant, the subsection to which you are referring, and (d) the date. The date is *not* the date the particular statute was passed. Use the year that appears on the spine of the code, or, the year that appears on the title page, or, the latest copyright year—in this order of preference. Where appropriate, you may also indicate the name of the statute or act at the beginning of the citation.

EXAMPLE

42 U.S.C. § 3412(a) (1970). *or* Narcotic Rehabilitation Act of 1966, 42 U.S.C. § 3412(a) (1970).

---

3. Statutes in the United States Statutes at Large are cited to (a) the volume in which the statute appears, (b) the abbreviated name of the compilation (Stat.), (c) the page number on which the statute begins, and (d) the date of the volume. Where appropriate, you may also indicate the name of the statute at the beginning of the citation.

EXAMPLE

80 Stat. 1444 (1966). *or* Narcotic Addict Rehabilitation Act of 1966, 80 Stat. 1444 (1966).

---

4. Recently enacted federal statutes which have not yet been published in U.S. Statutes at Large or the U.S.Code should be cited to (a) the public law number, (b) if relevant, the number of the particular title and section within the act, and (c) the exact date (day, month and year) of enactment. Where appropriate, you may also indicate the name of the statute at the beginning of the citation.

EXAMPLE

Narcotic Addict Rehabilitation Act of 1966, Pub.L. 80–793, Title III, § 302 (Nov. 8, 1966).

IV. Citing State Statutes

1. Like federal statutes, the statutes of the various states are compiled in two kinds of collections, state *codes* (arranged by subject matter), and *session laws* (arranged in chronological order of enactment).

2. Citations to state statutes should generally include (a) the title or chapter number of the statute, (b) the abbreviated name of the code or session laws, (c) the number of the section within the statute to which you are referring, and (d) the date. Use the year that appears on the spine of the code, or, the year that appears on the title page, or, the latest copyright year—in this order of preference.

3. For abbreviations and citation format, see the Uniform System of Citation (Blue Book).   It has a section for each state.

EXAMPLES

S.C. Code § 57.4(b) (1976)
Utah Code Ann. § 15 (1979)
D.C. Code Ann. § 45–2309 (1970)

V.   Citing Administrative Regulations

1. Federal administrative regulations are published in the *Federal Register* (Fed.Reg.) and are later codified by subject-matter in the *Code of Federal Regulations* (C.F.R.).

2. Federal regulations which appear in the *Code of Federal Regulations* are cited to (a) the title number in which the regulation appears, (b) the abbreviated name of the code, (c) the number of the particular section to which you are referring, and (d) the date of the code edition which you are using.

EXAMPLE

29 C.F.R. § 102.60(a) (1975).

---

3. Federal Regulations which have not yet been codified into the *Code of Federal Regulations* are cited to the *Federal Register* using (a) the volume in which the regulation appears, (b) the abbreviation "Fed.Reg.," (c) the page on which the regulation appears, and (d) the full date of the *Federal Register* which you are using.

EXAMPLE

27 Fed.Reg. 2092 (Mar. 3, 1962).

---

4. The regulations of state administrative agencies are rarely codified and the manner of citation may vary not only from state to state, but from agency to agency.   You should try to familiarize yourself with the system used by the agencies in your state and follow that system.

VI.   Citing the Documents of Legislative History[34]

1. The main sources of legislative history are (a) copies of the bills and amendments introduced, (b) copies of the reports and hearings of Congressional Committees, (c) the *Congressional Record* which contains transcripts of floor debates and material submitted from the floor, etc.

2. Bills and amendments are cited by referring to (a) the number assigned to the bill by the House or Senate and (b) the number and session of Congress during which the bill was introduced.

EXAMPLE

H.R. 1746, 92nd Cong., 1st Sess. *and* S. 2515, 92nd Cong., 1st Sess.

---

3. Reports of Congressional Committees are cited by reference to (a) the number of the report, (b) the number and session of the Congress during which the report was published, (c) the number of the page to which you are referring, and (d) the year in which the report was published.

EXAMPLE

H.R.Rep. No. 92–238, 92nd Cong., 1st Sess., 4 (1971) *and* S.Rep. No. 92–415, 92nd Cong., 1st Sess., 6 (1971).

---

4. Hearings held by Congressional Committees are cited by reference to (a) the title of the hearing, (b) the number and session of Congress during which the hearing was held, (c) the number of the page in the published transcript to which you are referring, and (d) the year in which the hearing was held.

EXAMPLE

Hearings before the Subcommittee on Labor of the Committee on Labor and Public Welfare of the United States Senate, 92nd Cong., 1st Sess., 315 (1971).

---

5. The Congressional Record is issued on a daily basis and later collected into bound volumes. The bound volumes may be cited by referring to (a) the number of the volume in which the item appears, (b) the abbreviation *Cong.Rec.*, (c) the number of the page on which the item appears, and (d) the year. The unbound daily volumes are cited in the same manner except that (a) the page number should be preceded by the letter "H" or "S" in order to indicate whether the item appeared in the House pages or the Senate pages of the volume, and (b) the date should include the exact day and month as well as the year.

EXAMPLE

Bound volumes: 103 Cong.Rec. 2889 (1957).
Unbound volumes: 22 Cong.Rec. S2395 (Feb. 26, 1976) *and* 122 Cong.Rec. H1385 (Feb. 26, 1976).

VII. Citing Secondary Authority

1. Treatises and other books are cited to (a) the number of the volume being referred to (if applicable), (b) full surname and first initial of the author, (c) the title of the book, (d) the number of the section and/or page to which you are referring, (e) the edition of the book, if other than the first, and (f) the date of publication. The title of the book should be italicized or underscored.

EXAMPLE

6 Belli, M., *Modern Trials,* § 289 (1963) *and* Osborne, G., *Handbook on the Law of Mortgages,* § 211, p. 370 (2d ed. 1970).

2. Law review *articles* are cited by reference to (a) the full surname and first initial of the author, (b) the title of the article, (c) the number of the volume in which the article appears, (d) the abbreviated name of the law review, (e) the number of the page on which the article appears, and (f) the date of publication.   The title of the article should be italicized or underscored.

EXAMPLE

Catz, R., and Robinson, E., *Due Process and Creditor's Remedies,* 28 Rutgers L.Rev. 541 (1975).

---

3. Law review *notes* and *comments* are cited in essentially the same manner as the law review articles (see #2, supra) except that the name of the author is omitted.

EXAMPLE

Second-Class Postal Rates and the First Amendment, 28 Rutgers L.Rev. 693 (1975).

---

4. Law review *case notes* are cited in essentially the same manner as law review articles (see #2, supra) except that both the name of the author and the title or heading of the case note are omitted.

EXAMPLE

28 Rutgers L.Rev. 720 (1975).

---

5. Legal Encyclopedias are cited by reference to (a) the number of the volume, (b) the abbreviated name of the encyclopedia, (c) the subject heading to which you are referring, (d) the number of the section to which you are referring, and (e) the date of publication of the volume you are citing.   When referring to a specific point within the section, you should, if possible, refer to the number of the footnote which corresponds to that point.   This reference should be inserted in your citation between the section number and the date of publication.

EXAMPLE

83 C.J.S., *Subscriptions* § 3, n. 32 (1953) *and* 77 Am.Jur.2d, *Vendor and Purchaser* § 73 (1975).

---

6. Restatements of the Law published by the American Law Institute are cited by reference to (a) the title of the Restatement, (b) the edition being referred to (if other than the first edition), (c) the number of the section being referred to, and (d) the date of publication.

EXAMPLE

Restatement, Agency 2d § 37 (1957).

Section K.   COMPONENTS OF A LAW BOOK

Law books have a definable style and format.   To be sure, there are some texts that are totally unique, e.g., Shepard's Citations.   In the main, however, there is a pattern to the texts.   The following is a list of components that are contained in many law books:

1. *Outside Cover.*
   Looking at the outside cover, you will find the title of the book, the author(s) or editor(s), the name of the publisher (usually at the bottom), the edition of the book (if more than one edition has been printed) and the volume (if the book is part of a series of books).   From a glance of the outside cover, the researcher should ask a number of important questions:
   a. Is it a book of law (written primarily by a court, a legislator or an administrator), or is it a book *about* the law (written by a scholar who is commenting on the law)?
   b. Is this book still operative?   Look at the books on the shelf in the area where you found the book that you are examining.   Is there a Replacement Volume for your book?   Is there a later edition of the book?

2. *Publisher's Page*
   Thumbing through the first few pages of the book, you will often find a page or pages about the publisher.   It may list other law books published by the same company.

3. *Title Page*
   The title page repeats most of the information contained on the outside cover: title, author, editor, publisher.   It also contains the date of publication.

4. *Copyright Page*
   On the copyright page (often immediately behind the title page) there is a copyright mark (©) plus a date or series of dates.   The most recent date listed indicates the timeliness of the material in the volume.   Given the great flux in the law, it is very important to determine how old the text is.   Generally, a book begins to become dated after the first four or five years.   The further back you go, the more out of date and useless the book might be.
   Note that if the book has a pocket-part (see below) it has been up-dated to the date on the pocket-part.

COPYRIGHT © 1971 through 1979 WEST PUBLISHING CO.

_____

COPYRIGHT © 1980
By
WEST PUBLISHING CO.

This dates on this copyright page indicate that the material in the book is current up to 1980, the latest copyright page.

5. *Authenticity Page*
   Books containing statutes and cases often have a page prepared by the Secretary of State or The Chief Judge of the Court indicating that the materials in the book are authentic.   These are usually official editions of the material. Of course, a book that does not have such a page is not to be considered

fraudulent. Unofficial editions prepared by private publishers have usually achieved great respectability and are used regularly. In some instances, courts and legislatures have adopted the private publisher's edition as the official edition for the jurisdiction and so indicate on the authenticity page.

6. *Forward or Preface or Explanation*

Under such headings, the reader will find some basic information about the book, particularly guidance on how the book was put together and how to use it.

7. *Summary Table of Contents*

On one or two pages, the reader can find the basic topics treated in the book.

8. *Detailed Table of Contents*

The detailed table can be very extensive. The major headings of the Summary Table are repeated plus detailed sub-headings and sub-sub-headings. This table is often used by researchers to determine where, if at all, they will find what they are after in the book. It is often a substitute for an index (see below).

9. *Table of Cases*

The text may list, alphabetically, every case, printed or referred to in the text with the page(s) where the case is found.

10. *Summary of Headnotes*[35]

If the volume contains reports of cases, there may be a number of pages with a listing of major headnotes drawn from those cases.

11. *Table of Statutes*

The text may list every statute treated or referred to in the text, plus the page numbers in the book where they appear. This table is sometimes found at the end of the book.

12. *List of Abbreviations*

The abbreviation list is critical and the reader who is new to law books should check the list immediately. It may be the only place in the book where the abbreviations used in the body of the text are spelled out. In *Shepard's Citations,* for example, the following abbreviations are found in the first few pages of their bound volumes and in most of their pamphlets covering case citations (a different abbreviation will be found for statutory citations):

```
History of Case
  a   (affirmed)        Same case affirmed on appeal.
  cc  (connected        Different case from case cited but arising out of same
        case)             subject matter or intimately connected therewith.
  D   (dismissed)       Appeal from same case dismissed.
  m   (modified)        Same case modified on appeal.
  r   (reversed)        Same case reversed on appeal.
  s   (same case)       Same case as case cited.
  S   (superseded)      Substitution for former opinion.
  v   (vacated)         Same case vacated.
  US cert den           Certiorari denied by U. S. Supreme Court.
  US cert dis           Certiorari dismissed by U. S. Supreme Court.
  US reh den            Rehearing denied by U. S. Supreme Court.
  US reh dis            Rehearing dismissed by U. S. Supreme Court.
Treatment of Case
  c   (criticised)      Soundness of decision or reasoning in cited case criticised
                          for reasons given.
  d   (distinguished)   Case at bar different either in law or fact from case cited
                          for reasons given.
  e   (explained)       Statement of import of decisions in cited case.  Not merely
                          a restatement of the facts.
  f   (followed)        Cited as controlling.
  h   (harmonized)      Apparent inconsistency explained and shown not to exist.
  j   (dissenting       Citation in dissenting opinion.
        opinion)
  L   (limited)         Refusal to extend decision of cited case beyond precise
                          issues involved.
  o   (overruled)       Ruling in cited case expressly overruled.
  p   (parallel)        Citing case substantially alike or on all fours with cited
                          case in its law or facts.
  q   (questioned)      Soundness of decision or reasoning in cited case ques-
                          tioned.
```

13. *Statutory History Table*

Sometimes there is a long or short table which will list every statute cited in the book and indicate whether it has been repealed or whether there is a new section number and title for the statute.   The legislature may have changed the entire name of the statutory chapter (e.g., from Prison Law to Corrections Law) and renumbered all of the sections.   Without this table, the researcher can become lost.   In the following example, note that former Prison Law sections 10–20 are now found in Correction Law sections 600–610.   The researcher may find a citation to a Prison Law section in a book which was published before the state changed to Correction Law sections. When s/he goes to look up the Prison Law Section, s/he may be lost unless s/he has a way to translate the section into a Corrections Law section.   The history table is one way to do it.

TABLE OF PRISON LAW SECTIONS

Showing the distribution of those sections of the former Prison Law in effect prior to the general amendment by L.1929, c. 243, which are contained wholly or in part in the Correction Law, or which have been omitted or re-pealed.

Prison Law Section	Correction Law Section
1	1
10–20	600–610
21	Repealed
22 L.1919, c. 12	611
22 L.1920, c. 983	612
23–32	613–622
40–50	40–50

---

14. *Body of the Text*

The fundamental characteristic of the body of most texts is that it is arranged according to divisions, sub-divisions, chapters, sub-chapters, parts, sub-parts, sections, sub-sections, etc.   Everything is usually numbered and sub-numbered.   The reader should thumb through the entire book to get a feel for the numbering and classification system used by the author or editor. The main exception to this structure is the reporter in which opinions are printed in rough chronological order rather than by divisions or sections.

15. *Footnotes*

Footnotes play a very important part in law books; researchers place great emphasis on them. Footnotes are often used to give extensive citations to cases and cross-references.

16. *Pocket-Parts*

A unique and indispensable feature of many law books are the pocket-parts. They are additions to the text placed at the very end of the text in a specially devised "pocket" built into the inside of the rear cover. The pocket-parts were published after the book was printed and are designed to bring the book up to date with the latest developments in the field covered by the book. Of course, pocket-parts can grow out of date also. Normally they are replaced every one or two years. The date of the pocket-part must be checked to see what period it covers. On the front cover of the pocket-part booklet, there will be large lettering telling the researcher what period is covered. Hence if the title page (see above) indicates that the last edition of the book was published in 1970 and the front page of the pocket-part says "for use during 1970–1972", the researcher can assume that the entire book contains the lastest material up to 1972. (Note that case reporters never have pocket-parts. Cases published subsequent to the date of the volume you are examining are always to be found in slip opinions and advance sheets [pamphlets] which are later consolidated into bound volumes).

Normally the organization of the pocket-part exactly parallels the organization of the main text. To find out if there has been anything new in the area covered by chapter 7, part 2, section 714, of the main text, for example, the reader goes to chapter 7, part 2, section 714 of the pocket-part. If nothing is found there, then nothing new has happened. If changes or additions have occurred, they will be found there.

Pocket-parts are cumulative[36] in that whenever a pocket-part is replaced by another pocket-part, everything in the early pocket-part is consolidated into the latter.

17. *Appendix*

The text may include one or more appendices. These could be on any number of topics. Normally, they will include tables, charts or the entire text of statutes or regulations, portions of which were discussed in the body of the book.

18. *Glossary-Dictionary*

The book may include a selected number of words used in the body of the text and defined in the glossary.

19. *Bibliography*

A brief or extended bibliography of the field covered by the book may be included at the end of each chapter or at the end of the book.

20. *Index-Specific*

The index is a critical part of the book. Unfortunately, some books either have no index or do a sloppy job of indexing (e.g., many sets of administrative regulations and loose-leaf services fall into this category). The index is arranged alphabetically and should refer the reader either to the page number(s) or the section number(s) where the item is treated in the body of the text.

The specific index is at the back of the book. If the book has two or three volumes, the index may be at the end of the last volume.

21. *General Index*

If there are a large number of volumes, there is often a separate series of volumes called "index," "general index" or "words and phrases." This broader index covers every volume in the series. The specific index to the individual volumes are consolidated within the general index.

Section L. THE CARTWHEEL: THE TECHNIQUE OF USING INDEXES AND TABLES OF CONTENT

We now come to one of the most important skills in legal research: the creative use of indexes and tables of contents in law books.[37] If you have this skill, 70% of the research battle is won. The CARTWHEEL is a technique designed to assist you in acquiring this skill.

The objective of the CARTWHEEL can be simply stated: to get you into the habit of trying to phrase every word involved in the client's problem *fifteen to twenty different ways!* When you go to the index or table of contents of a law book, you naturally begin looking up the words and phrases which you think should lead you to the relevant material in the book. If you do not find anything relevant to your problem, two conclusions are possible:

1. There is nothing relevant in the law book.
2. You looked up the wrong words in the index and table of contents.

Most people make the mistake of thinking that the first conclusion is accurate. Nine times out of ten, the second conclusion is the reason why the student fails to find material in the law book that was relevant to the problem of the client. The solution is to be able to phrase a word in as many different ways and in as many different contexts as possible. Hence, the CARTWHEEL.

In the center of the CARTWHEEL you place major words or phrases (one at a time) which come from the facts of the research problem. Each of these words or phrases are to be CARTWHEELED individually as demonstrated below. Suppose that your research problem involves a wedding. We now CARTWHEEL the word wedding:

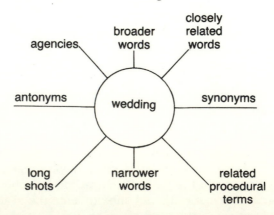

The first step in using the index and table of contents in any law book is to look up the word "wedding" in that index and table. Assuming that you are not successful with this word (either because the word is not in the index and table, or because the page or section references after the word in the index and table do not lead you to relevant material in the body of the book), the next step is to think of as many different phrasings and contexts of the word "wedding" as possible. Here is where the steps of the CARTWHEEL can be useful:

THE CARTWHEEL: USING THE INDEX AND TABLE OF CONTENTS OF LAW BOOKS

1. Identify all the *major words* from the facts of the client's problem (most of these facts can be obtained from the intake memorandum written following the initial interview with the client.) Place each word or small set of words in the center of the CARTWHEEL.
2. In the index and table of contents, look up all of these words.
3. Identify the *broader* categories of these major words.
4. In the index and table of contents, look up all of these broader categories.
5. Identify the *narrower* categories of these words.
6. In the index and table of contents, look up all of these narrower categories.
7. Identify all of the *synonyms* of these words.
8. In the index and table of contents, look up all of these synonyms.
9. Identify all of the *antonyms* of these words.
10. In the index and table of contents, look up all of these antonyms.
11. Identify all *closely related* words.
12. In the index and table of contents, look up all of these closely related words.
13. Identify all *procedural* terms related to these words.
14. In the index and table of contents, look up all of these procedural terms.
15. Identify all *agencies*, if any, which might have some connection to these words.
16. In the index and table of contents, look up all of these agencies.
17. Identify all *long shots*.
18. In the index and table of contents, look up all of these long shots.
   NOTE: The above categories are not mutually exclusive.

If we were to apply these 18 steps of the CARTWHEEL to the word "wedding," here are some of the words and phrases that would be checked in the index and table of contents of every law book that you examine:

BROADER WORDS: celebration, ceremony, rite, ritual, formality, festivity, etc.

NARROWER WORDS: civil wedding, church wedding, golden wedding, proxy wedding, sham wedding, shot-gun marriage, etc.

SYNONYMS: marriage, nuptial, etc.

ANTONYMS: alienation, annulment, divorce, separation, etc.

CLOSELY RELATED WORDS: matrimony, marital, domestic, husband, wife, bride, anniversary, custom, children, blood test, pre-marital, spouse, relationship, family, home, consummation, cohabitation, sexual relations, betrothal, minister, wedlock, oath, contract, name change, domicile, residence, etc.

PROCEDURAL TERMS: action, suit, statute of limitations, liability, court, complaint, discovery, defense, petition, jurisdiction, etc.

AGENCIES: Bureau of Vital Statistics, County Clerk, License Bureau, Secretary of State, Justice of the Peace, etc.

LONG SHOTS: dowry, common law, single, blood relationship, fraud, religion, license, illegitimate, remarriage, antenuptial, alimony, bigamy, pregnancy, gifts, chastity, community property, impotence, incest, virginity, support, custody, consent, paternity, etc.

There may be some overlapping of the categories; they are not mutually exclusive. Also, it is *not* significant whether you place a word in one category or another so long as the word comes to your mind as you comb through the index and table of contents. The CARTWHEEL is, in effect, a *word association game* which should become second nature to you with practice. Perhaps you might think that some of the word selections in the above categories are a bit farfetched. The problem, however, is that you simply will not know for sure whether a word will be fruitful until you try it. To be imaginative, one must be prepared to take some risks.

Indexes and tables of contents are often organized into headings, sub-headings, sub-sub-headings and perhaps even sub-sub-sub-headings. In the following excerpt from an index, "Burden of proof" is a sub-sub-heading of "Accidents" and a sub-heading of "Unavoidable accident or casualty." And the latter is a sub-heading of "Accidents" which is the main heading of the index entry.

> **Accidents**
>   Opportunity to avoid accident, application of last
>   clear chance doctrine, § 137(5), pp. 154–160
>   Parents' responsibility, attractive nuisance doc-
>   trine, § 63(76)
>   Pleading unavoidable accident as defense, § 197
>   Precautions against injury from dangerous place,
>   agency, etc., §§ 84–89, pp. 1016–1034
>   Presumption of negligence from happening, § 220.1,
>   pp. 506–512
>   Proximate cause of injury, § 115, pp. 1231–1234
>   Res ipsa loquitur, accident and defendant's rela-
>   tion thereto, §§ 220.10–220.15, pp. 551–578
>   Restaurant patron's injuries, liability, § 63(131)
>   Storekeeper's liability, § 63(121), p. 892
>   Unavoidable accident or casualty, § 21, pp. 647,
>   649
>   Burden of proof, § 204, p. 450, n. 86; § 209,
>   p. 482
>   Consistency between general verdict and find-
>   ings, § 304, p. 1072. n. 5

If you were looking for law on burden of proof, you may be out of luck unless you *first* thought of looking up accidents and unavoidable accident. Suppose that upon analysis of the facts of the problem you are researching you identify the following words that you want to check in the index:

minor	sale
explosion	warranty
car	damage

The index may have no separate heading for "minor," but "minor" may be a sub-heading under "sale." Be sure, therefore, to determine not only if the word has a separate heading, but also whether it is a sub-heading under the other words you are checking. Under each of the above six words, you should be alert to the possibility that the other five words may be sub-headings of that word. Hence the process of pursuing these six words in an index would be as follows (the word in capital letters is checked first and then the five words are checked under it to see if any of them are sub-headings);

CAR	DAMAGE	EXPLOSION
damage	car	car
explosion	explosion	damage
minor	minor	minor
sale	sale	sale
warranty	warranty	warranty

MINOR	SALE	WARRANTY
car	car	car
damage	damage	damage
explosion	explosion	explosion
sale	minor	minor
warranty	warranty	sale

ASSIGNMENT 2

One way to gain an appreciation for the use of indexes is to write one of your own.

1. Write a comprehensive index of your present job or the last job that you had.
2. Pick one area of the law that you have thus far covered in class or read about. Write your own comprehensive index on what you have learned.
3. Write a comprehensive index of the following statute:

§ 132. Amount of Force

The use of force against another for the purpose of effecting the arrest or recapture of the other, or of maintaining the actor's custody of him, is not privileged if the means employed are in excess of those which the actor reasonably believes to be necessary.

ASSIGNMENT 3

CARTWHEEL the following words or phrases:

1. Paralegal
2. Rat bite
3. Rear end collision
4. Monopoly

ASSIGNMENT 4

Examine the following index from Corpus Juris Secundum, a legal encyclopedia. It is an excerpt from the heading of Evidence. Death is the sub-heading of Evidence. What sub-sub-headings and/or sub-sub-sub-headings of Evidence would you check to try to find material on:

1. Introducing a death certificate into evidence.

2. The weight that a court will give to the personal conclusions of a witness.
3. Introducing the last words of the decedent into evidence.
4. A statement by the person who died that s/he did *not* own the land that s/he had placed a fence around.

EVIDENCE

Dealers,
    Securities, judicial notice, § 29, p. 890
Value,
    Household goods, opinion evidence, § 546(121), p. 479, n. 95
    Property, § 546(115), p. 430
        Opinion evidence, § 546(122), p. 483
Death,
    Autopsy, generally, ante
    Best evidence rule, § 803, p. 136
    Book entries,
        Entrant, proof of handwriting, § 693, p. 942
        Supplemental testimony respecting entries by clerks and third persons, § 693, p. 939
        Supporting entries by deceased persons by oath of personal representative, § 684, p. 910
    Clerk or employee making book entries, § 692
    Copy of record, certification by state registrar, § 664, p. 865, n. 69
    Declaration against interest, death of declarant, § 218, p. 604
    Declarations, § 227, p. 624
        Death of declarant as essential to admission, § 230
    Dying declarations, generally, post
    Experiments, object or purpose, § 588(1)
    Former evidence, death of witness, § 392
    General reputation, § 1048
    Hearsay, § 227, p. 624
        Death certificates, § 194, pp. 561, 562; § 766, p. 66
        Death of declarant, § 205
        Impossibility of obtaining other evidence, § 204
    Letters, § 703, p. 976
    Maps and diagrams of scenes of occurrence, § 730(1), p. 1045
    Memorandum, § 696, p. 955
    Mortality tables, generally, post
    Newspaper announcement, § 227, p. 625
    Opinion evidence,
        Animals, § 546(68)
        Cause and effect, § 546(11), p. 129
        Effect on human body, § 546(97), p. 374
        Fixing time, § 546(91), n. 16
    Owners, admissions, § 327
        Personal property, § 334
    Parol or extrinsic evidence, rule excluding, action to recover for, § 861, p. 230
    Photographs, personal appearance or identity, § 710
    Presumptions, ancient original public records, official making, § 746, p. 37
    Prima facie evidence, record of, § 644
    Private documents, recitals, § 677
    Public records and documents, registers of, § 623
    Reputation, § 227, p. 626
    Res gestae, statements, § 410, p. 991
    Rumor, § 227, p. 625
    Self-serving declarations, effect of death of declarant, § 216, p. 591
    Services, value, opinion evidence in death action, § 546(124), p. 489, n. 96
    Statements, weight of evidence, § 266
    Value of service rendered by claimant, opinion evidence, § 546(125), p. 493, n. 41

Death—Continued
    Witness, unsworn statements, circumstances tending to disparage testimony, § 268
    Wrongful death,
        Admissions, husband and wife, § 363
        Admissions of decedent, privity, § 322, n. 96.5
        Declarations against interest, § 218, p. 607
        Loss of life, value, opinion evidence, § 546(121), p. 473, n. 54
        Municipal claim, evidence of registry, § 680, n. 21
        Value of decedent's services, opinion evidence, § 546(124), p. 489, n. 96
Death certificates,
    Certified copies, § 651, p. 851
        Officer as making, § 664, p. 865, n. 69
        Prima facie evidence, § 773
    Church register, competency, § 727
    Conclusiveness, § 766, p. 64
    Expert testimony, supporting opinion, § 570
    Foreign countries, authenticated copies, § 675, p. 885
    Hearsay, § 194, pp. 561, 562; § 766, p. 66
    Kinship, § 696, p. 949, n. 2
    Official document, § 638, pp. 823, 824
    Prima facie case or evidence, post
Debate, judicial notice, United States congress, § 43, p. 995
Debs, judicial notice, § 67, p. 56, n. 17
Debtor and creditor, admissions, § 336
Debts. Indebtedness, generally, post
Decay,
    Judicial notice, vegetable matter, § 88
    Opinion evidence, buildings, § 546(73), p. 290
Decedents' estates,
    Judicial admissions, claim statements, § 310
    Judicial records, inferences from, § 765
    Official documents, reports and inventories of representatives, § 638, p. 818
    Value, opinion evidence, § 546(121), p. 478
Deceit. Fraud, generally, post
Decisions, judicial notice, sister states, § 18, p. 861
Declaration against interest, §§ 217–224, pp. 600–615
    Absence of declared from jurisdiction, § 218, p. 604
    Account, § 224
    Admissions, distinguished, § 217, p. 603
    Adverse character, § 222
    Affirmative proof as being best evidence obtainable, § 218, p. 604
    Apparent interest, § 219, p. 608
    Assured, § 219, p. 611
    Best evidence obtainable, necessity of, § 218, p. 604
    Boundaries, § 219, p. 611
    Coexisting, self-serving interest, § 221
    Contract, § 224
    Criminal prosecution, statement subjecting declarant to, § 219, p. 608
    Death action, § 218, p. 607
    Death of declarant, § 218, p. 605
    Dedication to public use, § 219, p. 611
    Deeds, § 224
    Disparagement of title § 219, p. 611
    Distinctions, § 217, p. 603
    Enrollment of vessel, § 224

Section M.   THE FIRST LEVEL OF LEGAL RESEARCH: BACKGROUND

There are three interrelated levels of researching a problem:

1. *Background Research*

To provide you with a general understanding of the area of law involved in your research problem.

2. *Specific Fact Research*

To provide you with primary and secondary authority that covers the specific facts of your research problem.

3. *Validation Research*

To provide you with the most up-to-date information on the current validity of all the primary authority on which you intend to rely in your research memorandum on the problem.

There are times when all three levels of research will be going on simultaneously. For someone new to legal research, however, it is recommended that you approach your research problem in the above three stages. Our concern in this section will be level I: background research. The other two levels will be covered throughout the remainder of the chapter.

Our assumption here is that you are researching a topic that is totally new to you, and/or that you are totally new to any field of law. It will be very helpful for you to spend an hour or two (depending on the complexity of the area) doing some reading in law books that will provide you with an overview of the area—a general understanding. This will help you identify the major terminology, the major agencies involved, if any, and some of the major issues. Of course, while doing this background research, you will probably also come up with leads that will be helpful in the second and third levels of research.

All of this background research will be in the secondary sources—legal encyclopedias, treatises, legal periodical literature, legal dictionaries, etc.[38] Caution must be exercised in studying these materials. They are no substitute for mandatory primary authority[39] which is the objective of your research. In your research memorandum, it will be rare for you to quote from a legal dictionary or a legal encyclopedia. Many courts do not consider them to be very persuasive. Treatises and legal periodical literature are considered somewhat more persuasive (depending upon who the author is), but, again, even these secondary sources should be infrequently quoted. Judges want to know what the primary authority is—opinions, statutes, constitutional provisions, regulations, etc. Use the secondary material for the limited purposes of (1) background reading, and (2) providing leads to primary authority—particularly through the footnotes of the secondary sources.

TECHNIQUES FOR DOING BACKGROUND RESEARCH ON A TOPIC

1. *Legal Dictionary.*[40]

Have access to a legal dictionary throughout your research. For example:

Black's Law Dictionary
Ballentine's Law Dictionary
Oran's Law Dictionary
Words and Phrases (West)

Look up the meaning of all key terms that you come across in your research. These dictionaries are starting points only. Eventually you want to find primary authority that defines these key terms.

TECHNIQUES—continued

TECHNIQUES—continued

2. *Legal Encyclopedias.*
   Go to the General Index of each of the major national legal encyclopedias:
   American Jurisprudence 2d [41]
   Corpus Juris Secundum [42]
   Also check any encyclopedias that cover only your state.   Use the CARTWHEEL to help you use their indexes and tables of contents.[43]

3. *Treatises.*[44]
   Go to your card catalog.   Use the CARTWHEEL to help you locate cards on treatises such as hornbooks, handbooks, formbooks, practice manuals, scholarly studies, etc.   Many of these books will have KF call numbers.   Use the CARTWHEEL to help you use the indexes and tables of contents of these books.

4. *Annotations.*
   Go to ALR, ALR2d, ALR3d, ALR4th and ALR Fed.[45]   Each of these sets of books have their own comprehensive indexes to annotations. Some of the sets also have a Quick Index.   Use the CARTWHEEL to help you use these indexes to find annotations on your topic.

5. *Legal Periodical Literature.*[46]
   Go to each of the three major indexes to legal periodical literature:
   Index to Legal Periodicals [47]
   Current Law Index [48]
   Regal Resource Index [49]
   Use the CARTWHEEL to help you use these indexes to locate legal periodical literature on your topic.

6. *Agency Reports/Brochures*
   If your research involves an administrative agency which is relatively close to you, call or write the agency.   Find out what brochures, reports or newsletters the agency has available to the public.   Such literature often provides useful background literature.

7. *Committee Reports*
   Before statutes are passed, committees of the legislature often write reports which comment on and summarize the legislation.   In addition to being good sources of legislative history on the statute,[50] the reports are excellent background reading.   If practical, contact both houses of the legislature to find out which committees acted on the statute.   If the statute is fairly recent, they may be able to send you copies of the committee reports or tell you where to obtain them.   Also check the law library of the legislature.   The committee reports of many federal statutes are printed in U.S. Code Congressional and Administrative News.[51]

8. *Reports/Studies of Special Interest Groups*
   There are special interest groups for almost every area of the law, e.g., unions, environment associations, tax associations, insurance company and other business associations.   They often have position papers and studies that they could send you.   Although one-sided, such literature should not be ignored.

9. *Martindale-Hubbell Law Directory*
   The Digest volume of Martindale-Hubbell [52] provides concise summaries of the law of the 50 states and many foreign countries.

Of course, you will not have time to check all of the above nine techniques to do the background research.   Usually one or two of the techniques will be sufficient for the limited purpose of providing you with an overview and of getting you started.

Section N.   CHECKLISTS FOR USING THE MAJOR SEARCH RESOURCES

We have said that the main objective of legal research is to locate mandatory primary authority.   There are three levels of government—federal, state, and local.   An overview of their primary authority is as follows:

FEDERAL LEVEL OF GOVERNMENT	STATE LEVEL OF GOVERNMENT	LOCAL LEVEL OF GOVERNMENT
U.S. Constitution Statutes of Congress Federal Court Opinions Federal Agency Regulations Federal Administrative Decisions Federal Rules of Court Federal Executive Orders Opinions of the U.S. Attorney General Treaties	State Constitution State Statutes State Court Opinions State Agency Regulations State Administrative Decisions State Rules of Court State Executive Orders Opinions of the State Attorney General	Charter Local Ordinances Local Court Opinions Local Agency Regulations Local Administrative Decisions Local Rules of Court Local Executive Orders Opinions of Corporation Counsel

Later in this chapter we will examine methods of finding most of the above kinds of primary authority.   Throughout that examination, you will be referred back to this section where ten checklists for the major finding tools are presented.   These ten finding tools (or search resources) are often useful for locating more than one kind of primary authority.   Hence they are presented together here.

Many of the ten search resources are also helpful in doing background research in the secondary sources.[53]   Indeed, some of the search sources *are* secondary sources themselves.   Finally, some of the search resources are also helpful in doing the third level of research—validation research, particularly Shepard's.[54]   In short, the following ten search resources or finding tools are the foundation of legal research itself:

1. Card Catalog
2. Digests
3. Annotations
4. Shepard's
5. Loose Leaf Services
6. Indexes to Legal Periodical Literature
7. Legal Encyclopedias
8. Treatises
9. Phone and Mail
10. Computers

1. CARD CATALOG

A well-organized card catalog is one of the researcher's best friends.   It is often an excellent place to begin your research.   Most law libraries use the Library of Congress classification system.   Many law books have KF call numbers under this system.   The following is an example of a card from a card catalog:

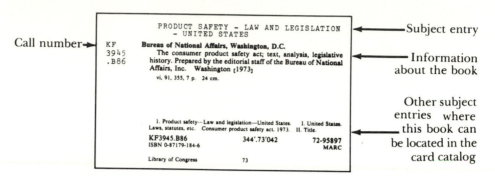

CHECKLIST #1

CHECKLIST FOR USING THE CARD CATALOG
1. Find out if your law library has more than one card catalog.   Is there a catalog with entries by subject matter and another with entries by author?   Are there different catalogs for different topics or areas of the law?
2. Find out if the library has any descriptive literature on how to use the catalog.
3. Pull out a tray at random from the catalog.   Thumb through the cards. Put a paper clip on an example of each kind of card that appears to be organized differently or that contains different kinds of information. Ask a librarian to spend ten minutes with you explaining the features of the cards that you have paper clipped.   (You should not remove the cards from the tray, but it may be possible in some libraries to bring the entire tray to the librarian.)
4. Be sure you understand all of the information on the cards that tell you where the books are located in the library.   Some books may be on reserve, in special rooms or in other buildings.
5. Select several cards at random, particularly where the books have different locations.   Go try to find these books.   Ask for help if you cannot locate them.
6. Now try the reverse process.   Select three different kinds of books from the shelves of the library at random.   (Not the same books you looked at in #5 above.)   Take these books to the card catalog and try to find the card for these books in the catalog.
7. Ask the librarian what kinds of research material, if any, are *not* located through the card catalog, e.g., microfilm, ultra fiche, appellate briefs, exams.
8. Ask the librarian what other lists of law books, if any, are in the library, e.g., lists of legal periodicals, lists of reserve books.

CHECKLIST—continued

CHECKLIST—continued

9. Ask the librarian to explain the difference between a card catalog and KARDEX (the latter is the place where many libraries keep records of current serial publications that come into the library every day). If your library does not use KARDEX, ask what it uses instead.
10. When using any card catalog, the CARTWHEEL will help you think of words and phrases to check. (Supra p. 70)
11. Never antagonize a law librarian! You are going to need all the help you can get!

ASSIGNMENT 5

On page 6 above it was suggested that you organize a system of 3 by 5 cards for each of the legal research words and phrases listed there. For each card that contains the name of a law look on it, find out where in the law library the book or set of books is located. Obtain this information from the card catalog. Enter the information on the card.

---

2. DIGESTS

We have already examined the major digests that exist and the names of the reporters whose opinions are summarized (in small paragraphs) in the digests. You should review this material now.[55]

Our focus here are the digests of West which are organized by the key number system. Lawyers Co-operative Publishing Company also has digests (for Supreme Court opinions [56] and for its annotations [57]) which are organized differently.

The beauty of the West digests is that once you know how to use one of the digests, you know how to use them all. A good way to begin this understanding is to follow the journey of a court opinion from the time it arrives at West Publishing Company in St. Paul:

JOURNEY OF A STATE COURT OPINION, e.g., CALIFORNIA	JOURNEY OF A FEDERAL COURT OPINION, e.g., A U.S. COURT OF APPEALS
(i) West editors write brief paragraph headnotes for the opinion. Each headnote summarizes a portion of the opinion.	(i) West editors write brief paragraph headnotes for the opinion. Each headnote summarizes a portion of the opinion.
(ii) The headnotes go at the beginning of the full text of the opinion in the reporter—here, the Pacific Reporter 2d (P.2d)	(ii) The headnotes go at the beginning of the full text of the opinion in the reporter—here, the Federal Reporter 2d (F.2d).
(iii) The editors assign each headnote a key topic and number, e.g., Criminal Law ☞ 1064(5).	(iii) The editors assign each headnote a key topic and number, e.g., Appeal and Error ☞ 1216.

JOURNEY OF A COURT OPINION—continued

JOURNEY OF A COURT OPINION—continued

(iv) This headnote is *also* printed in the appropriate digests of West. The above example will go in the "C" volume of the digest where "Criminal Law" is covered. The headnote will be placed under key number 1064(5) along with summaries of other opinions on the same or similar point of law.

(v) All headnotes go into the American Digest System. First, it goes into General Digest pamphlets and later into General Digest bound volumes. After a ten year period, all the General Digests are thrown away with the material in them printed in the next Decennial Digest.

(vi) All headnotes of Pacific Reporter 2d cases are *also* printed in its regional digest—the Pacific Digest.

(vii) All headnotes of California cases are *also* printed in the individual state digest—the California Digest.

(viii) Hence, the headnote from the California opinion will be printed:
—at the beginning of the opinion in P.2d
—in the American Digest System (first the General Digest and then the Decennial Digest)
—in the regional digest—Pacific Digest
—in the individual state digest—California Digest
In all of the above digests, the headnote will be printed in the "C" volume for Criminal Law under number 1064(5).

(iv) This headnote is *also* printed in the appropriate digests of West. The above example will go in the "A" volume of the digests where "Appeal and Error" is covered. The headnote will be placed under key number 1216 of Appeal and Error along with summaries of other opinions on the same or similar point of law.

(v) All headnotes go into the American Digest System. First, it goes into a General Digest pamphlet and later into a General Digest bound volume. After a ten year period, all the General Digests are thrown away with the material in them printed in the next Decennial Digest.

(vi) All headnotes of Federal Reporter 2d cases are *also* printed in the most current federal digest—the Federal Practice Digest 2d.

(vii) If our F.2d case dealt with a particular state, the headnotes of the F.2d case will *also* be printed in the individual state digest of that state.

(viii) Hence, the headnote from the opinion of the U.S. Court of Appeals will be printed:
—at the beginning of the opinion in F.2d
—in the American Digest System (first in the General Digest and then in the Decennial Digest)
—in the Federal Practice Digest 2d
—in an individual state digest if the F.2d case dealt with a particular state
In all of the above digests, the headnote will be printed in the "A" volume for Appeal and Error under number 1216.

All state court opinions printed in the reporters of West go through the same process as outlined in the first column above, e.g., opinions in A.2d, N.E.2d, N.W.2d, P.2d, S.E.2d, S.2d, S.W.2d. The exception would be step (v) above for N.E.2d opinions and for S.W.2d opinions. There is no regional digest that covers N.E.2d and S.W.2d.[58]

All U.S. District Court opinions printed in Federal Supplement (F.Supp.) go through the same process as outlined in the second column above. All

U.S. Supreme Court opinions printed in Supreme Court Reporter (S.Ct.) also go through the same process as outlined in the second column above. For Supreme Court cases, however, there is an additional digest where all their headnotes are printed—the U.S. Supreme Court Digest of West.[59]

Assume that you are doing research on the right of a citizen to speak in a public park. You find that the digests of West cover this subject under the following key topic and number:

Constitutional Law ⟜ 211

West publishes about 60 digests—state, federal and national. You can go to the "C" volume of *any* of these 60 digests, turn to "Constitutional Law" and find number "211" under it. Do you only want Idaho case law? If so, go to Constitutional Law ⟜ 211 in the Idaho Digest. Do you only want case law from the states in the western United States? If so, go to Constitutional Law ⟜ 211 in the Pacific Digest. Do you only want federal case law? If so, go to Constitutional Law ⟜ 211 in the Federal Practice Digest 2d. Do you only want U.S. Supreme Court cases? If so, go to Constitutional Law ⟜ 211 in the U.S. Supreme Court Digest (West). Do you want the case law of *every* court in the country? If so, trace Constitutional Law ⟜ 211 through the American Digest System:

- go to Constitutional Law ⟜ 211 in every bound and unbound General Digest
- go to Constitutional Law ⟜ 211 in every Decennial Digest
- go to Constitutional Law ⟜ 211 (or its equivalent number) in the Century Digest

To trace a key topic and number through the American Digest System means to find out what case law, if any, is summarized under that key topic and number in every unit of the American Digest System.

CHECKLIST #2

CHECKLIST FOR USING THE DIGESTS OF WEST
1. Step one is to locate the right digests for your research problem. This is determined by identifying the kind of case you want to find. State? Federal? Both? Review pages 28 ff. on the American Digest System, the five regional digests, the three major federal digests, the two digests for U.S. Supreme Court cases (only one of which is a West digest) and the 50 individual state digests. You must know what kind of case law is contained in each of these digests. See the chart on page 32.
2. Step two is to find a key topic and number to cover your research problem. There are thousands of topics and sub-topics in the digests. How do you find the ones relevant to your research problem? There are four techniques: (i) Descriptive Word Index (DWI). Every digest has a DWI. Use the CARTWHEEL (supra p. 70) to help you locate key topics and numbers in the DWI. (ii) Table of Contents. There are approximately 400 main topics in the West digests. These topics are listed in the tables of contents of the West digests. These tables of contents have different names: "Scope Note", "Analysis", or "Subjects Included". Use the CARTWHEEL to help you locate key topics and numbers in the table of contents.

CHECKLIST #2—continued

> (iii) Headnote in West Reporter. Suppose that you already have an opinion on point. You are reading its full text in a West reporter. Go to the headnotes at the beginning of this opinion. Each headnote has a key topic and number. Use this key topic and number to go to any of the digests to find *more* case law on that topic and number.
>
> (iv) Table of Cases in the Digests. Suppose again that you already have an opinion on point. You are reading its full text in any reporter. Go to the Table of Cases in the American Digest System and/or in any other digest that covers the reporter. Look up the name of the case in this Table of Cases. There you will find out what key topics and numbers that case is digested under in the digest. Go to that topic and number in the body of the digest to find that case summarized as well as other cases on the same topic and number. (Note: the Table of Cases in some West digests are listed as Plaintiff-Defendant Tables or as Defendant-Plaintiff Tables depending on which party's name comes first. The Defendant-Plaintiff Table is useful if you happen to know only the name of the defendant or if you want many cases where the same party was sued, e.g., General Motors. Defendant-Plaintiff Tables usually refer you back to the Plaintiff-Defendant Table where the key topics and numbers are listed.)
>
> The Table of Cases in the digests can also provide you with a parallel cite to the case, supra p. 59.

3. While using the Descriptive Word Index (DWI) in any of the digests, you may come across a key topic and number that appears to be relevant to your research problem. When you go to check that topic and number in the body of the digest, however, you might find no case law and the phrase "See Scope Note for Analysis." The index has, in effect, led you to non-existent case law! The editors are telling you that there are no cases digested under this topic and number at this time. Go to the Table of Contents for the main topic you are in. Check the Scope Note and Analysis there to see if you can find a more productive key topic and number.

4. The West editors are adding new key topics and numbers all the time. Hence, you may find topics and numbers in the later digests that are not in the earlier digests.

5. The first key number under most topics and sub-topics are often labeled "In General." This is obviously a broad category. Many researchers make the mistake of overlooking it in their quest for more specific topic headings.

6. The West digests obviously duplicate each other in some respects. The American Digest System, for example, contains everything that is in all the other digests. A regional digest will duplicate everything found in the individual state digest covered in that region. (See the chart on page 32.) It is wise, nevertheless, to check more than one digest. Some digests may be more up to date than others in your library. You may miss something in one digest that you will catch in another.

7. Be sure you know all the units of the most comprehensive digest—the American Digest System: Century Digest, Decennial Digests, General Digests. (See page 29.) These units are distinguished solely by the period of time covered by each unit. Know what these periods of time are. Century Digest (1658–1896). Decennial Digests (ten year periods). General Digests (the period since the last digest was printed).

8. At the time the Century Digest was printed, West had not invented the key number system. Hence topics are listed in the Century Digest by section

CHECKLIST #2—continued

> numbers rather than key numbers.   There is a parallel table in volume 21 of the First Decennial which will tell you the corresponding key topic number for any section number in the Century Digest.   Suppose, however, you have a key topic and you want to find out its corresponding section number in the Century Digest?   In the First and Second Decennial, there is a "see" reference under the key topic number which will tell you the corresponding section number in the Century Digest.

> 9. Tricks of the trade are also needed in using the General Digests which cover the most recent period since the last Decennial Digest was printed. When the current ten year period is over, all the General Digests will be thrown away and cumulated into the next Decennial Digest.   When you go to use the General Digests, there may be 50–60 bound volumes and 5–6 pamphlets.   To be thorough in tracing a key topic and number in the General Digest, you must check *all* bound volumes and pamphlets.   There is, however, one shortcut.   Look for the "Cumulative Table of Key Numbers" within bound and unbound General Digests.   This Table tells you which General Digests contain anything under the key topic number you are searching.   You do not have to check the other General Digests. There will be more than one such table covering different clusters of General Digest volumes (referred to as "Series").   Find all of these Tables to use this shortcut.   (You will not need this shortcut in checking a key topic number in the Decennial Digests—you have to check the key topic number in a Decennial only once.)

3.   ANNOTATIONS

The main meaning of annotation is notes or commentary on something.[60] The most extensive annotations are those of the Lawyers Co-operative Publishing Co.:[61]

ALR: American Law Reports, First

ALR2d: American Law Reports, Second

ALR3d: American Law Reports, Third

ALR4th: American Law Reports, Fourth

ALR Fed: American Law Reports, Federal

All five sets of books are reporters in that they print opinions in full.   They are annotated reporters in that notes or commentary is provided after each case in the form of an annotation.   The following is an example of an annotation found on page 1015, volume 91 of ALR3d (cited as 91 ALR3d 1015):

ANNOTATION

LIABILITY OF TELEGRAPH OR TELEPHONE COMPANY FOR TRANSMITTING OR PERMITTING TRANSMISSION OF LIBELOUS OR SLANDEROUS MESSAGES

§ 1. Introduction:
  [a] Scope
  [b] Related matters
§ 2. Liability of telegraph company for transmission of customer's messages:
  [a] Generally
  [b] Privilege
§ 3. Liability of telegraph company for transmission of own messages
§ 4. Liability of telephone company for defamatory telephone call

§ 1. Introduction

[a] Scope
  It is the purpose of this annotation¹ to collect the cases discussing the liability of a telegraph or telephone company for transmitting or permitting transmission of libelous or slanderous messages.
  Cases involving the question whether a telegraph company could be subjected to punitive damages because of the transmission of a libelous message are excluded from this annotation.

[b] Related matters
  Defamation by radio or television. 50 ALR3d 1311.

  Liability of a Telegraph Company for Transmitting a Defamatory Message. 20 Col L. Rev 30, 369.

The annotations are based on issues in the limited number of opinions that the editors print in full immediately before the annotations. Some annotations are over 50 pages long. A researcher is in heaven when s/he finds an annotation that covers the research problem being worked on. The joy is somewhat similar to finding a key topic and number in the West digests that is on point.[62] In fact, West's key number system in the digests is the major rival and competitor of the annotations of Lawyers Co-op as a case-finding technique for the researcher. Because of the tremendous number of annotations that exist, you are given access to hundreds of thousands of cases in the annotations. You are given access to an equal number of cases through the West digests. In looking for case law, it is always wise to check the digests *and* the annotations.

The annotations in the five sets cover both federal and state law. ALR First, ALR2d and most of ALR3d cover both state and federal law. The later volumes of ALR3d and all of ALR4th cover mainly state law. ALR Fed covers only federal law. The annotations in these five sets do not follow any particular order. There may be an annotation on attempted burglary followed, for example, by an annotation on defective wheels on baby carriages. The annotations in ALR First and ALR2d are older than the annotations in ALR3d, ALR4th and ALR Fed, but this is not significant because all of the annotations can be updated.

The use of the five sets of annotations raises two questions:

1. How do you find an annotation on point?
2. How do you update an annotation that you have found?

The answers to these questions are a bit cumbersome. Unfortunately, many researchers are scared away from the five sets because of their awkward indexing and updating features. Do not let this happen to you. As indicated earlier, the annotations contain a goldmine of research that is already done for you. The indexing and updating features of the five sets may be awkward, but it is well worth your while to learn what they are. Once you know them and begin using the sets, any initial confusion will disappear. Furthermore, Lawyers Co-op invented some features for ALR3d, ALR4th and ALR Fed which make them a little more easy to use than the earlier ALR First and ALR2d.

(1) Finding an Annotation On Point

The indexing features of ALR First and ALR2d are similar. Each set has three index systems:

INDEX SYSTEMS FOR ALR First	INDEX SYSTEMS FOR ALR2d
• Quick Index	• Quick Index
• Word Index to Annotations	• Word Index to Annotations
• Permanent Digest of ALR Annotated	• ALR2d Digest

You should use each of the three index systems in the order listed above. And use all three. Do not walk away, for example, if the Quick Index appears to have nothing on point. Go on to the more comprehensive Word Index and Digest for the set. Also, use the three index systems for both sets—a total of six indexes.

Within the digests there are *tables of cases* which list the cases selected to be printed in full. If you want to know whether a particular court opinion (which you already have in another reporter) is also found in ALR First or ALR2d, check the table of cases in their respective Digests. Similar tables of cases exist in recent Quick Index volumes. These tables of cases, however, are less productive as research tools than the three index systems themselves.

What about the index systems for ALR3d, ALR4th and ALR Fed? Find the Quick Indexes that cover these sets. Look on the front binding of all Quick Indexes to determine which sets they cover. One of the Quick Indexes may be called Quick Index to Total Client-Service Library which will give you access to more than one of the five sets, plus references to other books by the same publisher, e.g., Am Jur 2d,[63] L.Ed.[64] etc. The Quick Index volumes are undergoing change and development. Lawyers Co-op, for example, may have a Quick Index that covers more than one of the five sets.

Also, look for Word Indexes and Digests for ALR3d, ALR4th and ALR Fed. These sets may still be growing and the publisher may wait until the last volume of the set has been printed before putting out Word Indexes and Digests for them. In fact, by the time you use the sets, the publisher may have invented altogether new index features.

The last point is particularly important. Someday there may be an ALR5th, ALR6th, etc. Be flexible enough to expect "new and improved" index systems for the sets.

There is in a special volume called ALR Fed. Tables of Cases, Laws, Regs which contains a table you should never forget when researching federal law: Table of Laws and Regulations Cited in ALR Fed. This table will tell you whether there is an annotation on a specific federal statute in U.S.C.[65] or a specific federal regulation in C.F.R.[66] you may be examining. The volume also has a table of cases which will tell you what federal cases were the bases of annotations printed in ALR Fed.

Having used the above index systems and located an annotation on point, look for the equivalent of tables of content and further indexes at the beginning of the individual annotations. Particularly helpful is the Table of Jurisdictions Represented which will tell you where the law of a particular state is discussed within the annotation. This is found in ALR3d and ALR4th. In ALR Fed there is a Table of Courts and Circuits which will tell you where the law of particular federal courts is discussed within the annotation.

TABLE OF JURISDICTIONS REPRESENTED			TABLE OF COURTS AND CIRCUITS	
Consult POCKET PART in this volume for later cases			Consult POCKET PART in this volume for later cases and statutory changes	
US: §§ 2[b], 3, 4[a], 5[b], 6[a], 7[a], 10[b]	Miss: §§ 4[a]		Sup Ct: §§ 2[a], 3[a], 5, b, 14	Sixth Cir: §§ 5[b], 6[b], 10[a, b], 12[a], 13[a], 15[b]
Ala: §§ 2[b], 4[a], 6[a], 7[a], 8, 10[b]	Mo: §§ 4[a], 6[a], 10[b]		First Cir: §§ 5[b], 6[b], 15[b], 16[a], 18[a]	Seventh Cir: §§ 2[a, b], 4[b], 5[b], 10[b], 15[b]
Cal: §§ 4[a, b], 7[a, b], 10[b], 11	NH: §§ 3, 4[b]		Second Cir: §§ 2[b], 3[a, b], 5[a], 12[a], 16[a], 18[a]	Eighth Cir: §§ 3[a], 4[a, b], 5[a, b], 6[a], 12[a], 13[a], 15[b], 16[a], 17, 19
Fla: §§ 5[a]	NC: §§ 7[a]		Third Cir: §§ 3[a], 5[a], 7, 11[b], 12[b], 13[a], 15[b]	Ninth Cir: §§ 2[a, b], 3[a], 4[a], 5, a, 6[b], 7, 8, 10[a], 11[a, b], 12[a, b], 13[a, b], 15[a, b], 16[b], 17, 18[a, b]
Ga: §§ 3, 4[b], 5[b], 6[b], 10[a]	Ohio: §§ 4[a, b], 6[a], 7[a, b], 10[b]			
Ill: §§ 4[b], 5[a, b], 6[a, b], 10[a]	Or: §§ 4[a], 10[b]			
Ind: §§ 4[a], 5[b], 6[a], 7[a, b], 8, 9, 10[b]	Pa: §§ 4[a], 7[a], 10[b]		Fourth Cir: §§ 2[b], 3[a], 4[b], 5[a, b], 8, 9, 10[b], 12[a, b], 13[b], 14, 15[a, b], 16[a], 17, 18[a]	Tenth Cir: §§ 2[b], 3[a], 5[a, b], 6[a, b], 9, 11[a, b], 12[a], 14, 17, 18[b]
Iowa: §§ 7[a], 8	Tenn: §§ 4[a], 5[b], 6[a]			
Ky: §§ 3, 4[a], 5[b]	Tex: §§ 4[a], 7[a], 10[b]		Fifth Cir: §§ 3[a], 5[a, b], 8, 10[a], 11[a, b], 13[a], 15[a], 16[b], 18[b]	Dist Col Cir: §§ 3[b], 5[b], 6[b], 10[a, b]
La: §§ 5[b], 7[a, b]	Vt: §§ 9			Ct Cl: § 16[a]
Me: §§ 5[b], 7[a], 10[b]	Wash: §§ 6[a], 7[a], 8			
Md: §§ 4[b]	Wis: §§ 7[a], 8, 10[b], 11			
Mich: §§ 4[a], 10[b]				

(2) Updating an Annotation

Let us assume that you have found an annotation in one of the five sets. That annotation is current only up to the date of the particular volume in which the annotation is found. How do you bring the annotation up to date? How do you find more recent law on the topics of the annotation?

The answer is simple for annotations in ALR3d, ALR4th and ALR Fed: simply check the pocket part of the volume where the original annotation was found.   The answer is not simple for annotations in ALR First and ALR2d.

How to Update an Annotation in ALR First	*How to Update an Annotation in ALR 2d*
Check *every* volume of the ALR Blue Book of Supplemental Decisions [67]	Check the volumes (and pocket parts) of ALR 2d Later Case Service which cover the cite of the annotation you want updated

If the volumes of ALR First and ALR 2d had pocket parts (which they do not), there would be no need for the ALR Blue Book of Supplemental Decisions, nor the ALR 2d Later Case Service.

Finally, you must check the Annotations History Table.   This table will tell you if there is a supplemental annotation for the annotation you are examining.   A supplemental annotation totally updates an earlier annotation. The table also directs you to superseded annotations which totally replace earlier annotations.   To find this Annotation History Table, check the Quick Index volumes.   There may be more than one such table.

Note on Another Annotated Reporter of Lawyers Co-op

Lawyers Co-op also publishes United States Supreme Court Reports, Lawyers Edition (abbreviated L.Ed).[68]   This is also an annotated reporter in that it prints the full text of opinions (those of the U.S. Supreme Court) with annotations on issues following some of these opinions.

CHECKLIST #3

CHECKLIST FOR FINDING AND UPDATING ANNOTATIONS IN ALR, ALR2d, ALR3d, ALR4th AND ALR FED
1. Your goal is to use all five sets to find annotations on your research problem. The annotations are extensive research papers on numerous points of law.
2. If you already have the cite of an opinion, find out if Lawyers Co-op printed it in full and wrote an annotation on it.   Check the table of cases in any of the digest volumes and in some of the Quick Index volumes of the sets. (For recent federal cases, check the separate volume called ALR Fed. Tables of Cases, Laws, Regs.)
3. If you do not have a case to start with, find all the Quick Index volumes on the shelves for all the sets.   Use the CARTWHEEL (supra p. 70) to help you locate annotations in these Quick Index volumes.
4. Also use the more comprehensive Word Indexes for the sets.   (For some sets, the Word Index may not have been published yet.)   Use the CARTWHEEL to help you locate annotations in these Word Indexes.
5. Also use the more comprehensive Digests for the sets.   (For some sets, the Digests may not have been printed yet—or may have been discontinued.) Use the CARTWHEEL to help you locate annotations in the Digests.
6. If you already have the cite of a federal statute or a federal regulation, find out if there are annotations on it.   Check the subject matter of the statute through the above three index systems (##3, 4, and 5 above) and check the following table: Table of Laws and Regulations cited in ALR Fed.   This table is in the separate volume called ALR Fed. Tables of Cases, Laws, Regs.

CHECKLIST #3—continued

CHECKLIST #3—continued

7. Once you have been led to an annotation through steps ## 2–6 above, use the indexes or tables of contents at the beginning of the annotation itself to help you locate specific sections of the annotation. (Use the CARTWHEEL for these internal indexes).

8. Once you have an annotation, you must update it. Updating features differ depending on the set in which the annotation is found:
   (a) To update annotations in ALR First:
      —check every volume of the ALR Blue Book of Supplemental Decisions
      —check the Annotation History Table (e.g., in one of the Quick Indexes)
   (b) To update annotations in ALR 2d:
      —check the volume of ALR2d Later Case Service that covers the cite of your annotation
      —check the pocket part of this volume of ALR2d Later Case Service
      —check the Annotation History Table
   (c) To update annotations in ALR3d, ALR4th and ALR Fed:
      —check the pocket part of the volume where the annotation is found
      —check the Annotation History Table

9. Guideline #2 above assumed that you began your search with the cite of a case. Suppose that the case was decided by the U.S. Supreme Court. Also check to see if an annotation was written on that case in L.Ed.–United States Supreme Court Reports, Lawyers Edition, which is an annotated reporter by the same publisher.

4. SHEPARD'S

There are four great research inventions in the law:

- The Key Number System of the West Digests [69]
- The Annotations in ALR, ALR2d, ALR3d, ALR4th and ALR Fed [70]
- Computers [71]
- Shepard's

Among the functions served by these four systems is case finding; they are all excellent ways of finding case law. In a sense, they duplicate each other for this function.

   We now turn to Shepard's and the techniques of *shepardizing*. You should review the material on pages 41–45 covering the kinds of Shepard's volumes that exist, the material on page 59 covering the use of Shepard's as one of the four techniques of finding a parallel cite, and the material on page 14 describing an advance sheet for Shepard's.

   Shepard's is a citator which means that its function is to provide you with relevant citations to whatever you are shepardizing. Our concern here is what these relevant citations are and how you locate them in Shepard's. Specifically, we shall cover:

1. The units of a set of Shepard's
2. Determining whether you have a complete set of Shepard's ("reading the box")
3. The distinction between "Cited Material" and "Citing Material"
4. Abbreviations in Shepard's
5. Shepardizing a case (court opinion)
6. Shepardizing a statute
7. Shepardizing a regulation

We will limit ourselves to shepardizing cases, statutes and regulations. Knowing how to shepardize these items will equip you to shepardize other items as well (e.g., constitutions, administrative decisions, charters, rules of court, etc.)

1. The Units of a Set of Shepard's

By "set of Shepard's" we mean those volumes of Shepard's which cover a specific reporter, statutory code, administrative code or whatever else is being shepardized. There are two main units to every set of Shepard's: (a) bound red volumes, and (b) white, gold, yellow or red pamphlet volumes. The bound volumes and pamphlets are sometimes broken into Parts, e.g., Part 1, Part 2, etc. The white pamphlet is the advance sheet [72] which is later thrown away and cumulated (or consolidated) into a larger pamphlet. Eventually all the pamphlets are thrown away and cumulated into bound red volumes. The pamphlets contain the most current shepardizing material.

2. Determining whether you have a Complete Set of Shepard's ("Reading the Box")

You should never try to shepardize until you have satisfied yourself that there is a complete set of Shepard's on the shelf in front of you. As we saw above, Shepard's comes in sets, e.g., the set of Shepards for United States statutes, the set for New Mexico laws, etc. You must have a complete set in order to shepardize anything. To determine whether you are complete, go through the following five steps:

1. Pick up the advance sheet or the latest dated pamphlet for that set of Shepard's (the date is on the top of the pamphlet).
2. What month and year is at the top of this advance sheet or other pamphlet? If the month is not the month of today's date or the immediately preceding month, ask the librarian what is the date of the most recent pamphlet the library has received for the set of Shepard's you are using. (The librarian will check the office KARDEX or other system of recording what the library has received.)
3. Once you are satisfied yourself that the advance sheet or latest pamphlet is the most current the library has, go to the box on its front cover. You must now read this box. It will tell you what is a complete set of Shepard's for the set you are using. Go down the list in the box and satisfy yourself that the library has on its shelf everything the box tells you should be there.
4. The last entry in the box is always the advance sheet or other pamphlet that contains that box.
5. If you do not have a complete set of Shepard's according to the box, stop! It is close to useless to do an incomplete job of shepardizing. If you do not have everything the box commands, you are incomplete.

Here is the box on the cover of the set of Shepard's that will allow you to shepardize Hawaii cases:

What Your Library Should Contain
1960 Bound Volume
Supplemented with
Oct. 1980 Cumulative Supplement Vol. 21 No. 3
Destroy All Other Issues

To be complete, there must be a 1960 Bound Volume of Hawaii Shepard's and an October 1980 Cumulative Supplement for Hawaii Shepard's (vol. 21, no. 3).   The last entry is the pamphlet on which the above box is located.

We now examine a more complicated box.   On page 90 you will find a box from Shepard's Federal Citations.   This unit of Shepard's comes in two parts: Part 1 for the shephardizing of Federal Reporter cases, and Part 2 for shepardizing Federal Supplement cases.

If you are shepardizing a case you found in the Federal Reporter:

If you are shepardizing a case you found in the Federal Supplement:

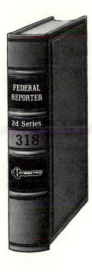

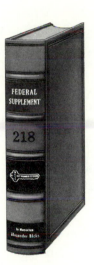

To be complete you must have the following units of Shepard's on the shelf:
__ A 1969 bound volume
__ A second 1969 bound volume
__ A third 1969 bound volume
__ A 1969–1977 bound volume
__ A 1977 bound volume
__ Part 1A, July, 1980 Semiannual Supplement (vol. 70, no. 4)
__ Part 1B, July, 1980 Semiannual Supplement (vol. 70, no. 4)
__ Part 1, Oct., 1980 Cumulative Supplement (vol. 70, no. 7)
__ Part 1, Dec., 1980 Cumulative Supplement (vol. 70, no. 9)

To be complete you must have the following units of Shepard's on the shelf:
__ A 1969 bound volume
__ A 1969–1975 bound volume
__ Part 2, July, 1980 Semiannual Supplement (vol. 70, no. 4)
__ Part 2, Oct., 1980 Cumulative Supplement (vol. 70, no. 7)
__ Part 2, Dec., 1980 Cumulative Supplement (vol. 70, no. 9)

Part I covers cases in the Federal Reporter.   Part II covers cases in the Federal Supplement.

What Your Library Should Contain

PART 1	PART 2
(Covering	(Covering
Federal Reporter	Federal Supplement,
and Federal Cases)	FRD, Court of Claims)
(3) 1969 Bound Volumes	(1) 1969 Bound Volume
(1) 1969–77 Bound Volume	(1) 1969–75 Bound Volume
(1) 1977 Bound Volume	

Supplemented with
July, 1980 Semiannual Supplement Vol. 70 No. 4
(Parts 1A, 1B and 2)

Oct., 1980 Cumulative Supplement Vol. 70 No. 7
(Parts 1 and 2)

Dec., 1980 Cumulative Supplement Vol. 70 No. 9
(Parts 1 and 2)

Destroy All Other Issues

If you cannot check off all of the items for either column (depending on whether you are shepardizing a F.2d case or a F.Supp. case), then you do not have a complete set of Shepard's with which to proceed.

Finally, be alerted to the fact that some sets of Shepard's cover cases and statutes within the same units, while other sets are subdivided into case volumes and statute volumes within the same set of Shepard's. Again, let the box be your guide.

3. The Distinction between "Cited Material" and "Citing Material"

Cited Material: whatever you are shepardizing, e.g., a case, statute, regulation

Citing Material: whatever mentions or discusses the cited material, e.g., another case, a law review article, an annotation in ALR, ALR2d, ALR3d, ALR4th, ALR Fed, etc.

Suppose you are shepardizing the case found in 75 F.2d 107 (a case that begins on page 107 of volume 75 of Federal Reporter 2d). While reading through the columns of Shepard's, you find the following cite: f56 S.E.2d 46. The cited material is 75 F.2d 107. The citing material is 56 S.E.2d 46 which followed (f) or agreed with the decision in 75 F.2d 107.

Suppose you are shepardizing a statute: 22 U.S.C. § 55.8 (section 55.8 of title 22 of the United States Code. While reading through the columns of Shepard's, you find the following cite: 309 U.S. 45. The cited material is 22 U.S.C. § 55.8. The citing material is 309 U.S. 45 which interpreted or mentioned 22 U.S.C. § 55.8.

Shepard's always indicates the cited material by the black bold print along the top of every page of Shepard's and by the black bold print numbers that are the volume or section numbers of the cited material. In the following excerpt, the cited material is 404 P.2d 460 indicated by the first arrow. The citing material follows the number 460:

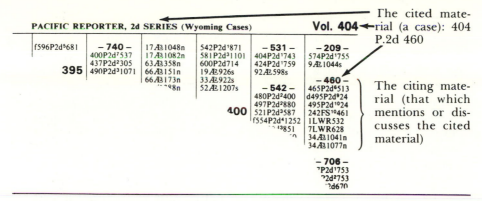

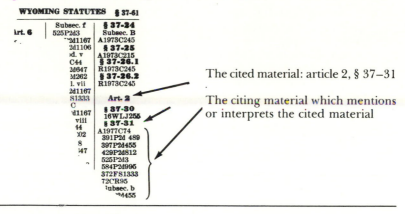

In the following excerpt, the cited material is a statute: Article 2, § 37–31 of the Wyoming Statutes. The citing material is indicated beneath § 37–31.

4. The Abbreviations in Shepard's

Shepard's packs a tremendous amount of information (the cites) onto every one of its pages. Each page contains about eight columns of cites for the cited and the citing materials. For the sake of economy, Shepard's uses many abbreviations which are peculiar to Shepard's. For example:

FS→means Federal Supplement

*→means that a regulation of a particular year was discussed

A³ →means American Law Reports 3d

Δ→means that a regulation was discussed without mentioning the year of the regulation

It would be impossible for the ordinary researcher to know the meaning of every abbreviation and signal used by Shepard's. *But you must know where to find their meaning.* There are two places to go:

- In the abbreviations tables at the beginning of most of the units of Shepard's (for an example, see supra p. 68)
- In the preface or explanation pages found at the beginning of most of the units of Shepard's

Many researchers neglect the latter. Buried within the preface or explanation pages may be the interpretation of the abbreviation or symbol which was not covered in the abbreviations tables.

5. *Shepardizing a Case (Court Opinion)*

In order to shepardize a case, you must have a citation to the case—you must know the reporter in which the case is printed in full. The Shepard's volumes that enable you to shepardize cases correspond to the reporter volumes for those cases. For example, if the case you want to shepardize is 193 Mass. 364, you know that the name of the reporter is Massachusetts Reports (which is what "Mass." means). Hence, to shepardize this case, you go to Shepard's Massachusetts Citations. If the case you want to shepardize is 402 F.2d 1065, you know that the name of the reporter is Federal Reporter 2d (which is what F.2d means). To shepardize this case, you go to the Shepard's set that covers F.2d cases—Shepard's Federal Citations. Almost every reporter has a corresponding Shepard's set which will enable you to shepardize cases in that reporter.[73]

Of course, many cases have parallel cites—the case is found word-for-word in more than one reporter. You can shepardize the case through *either* reporter for most cases with parallel cites. Assume you want to shepardize the following case:

Welch v. Swasey, 193 Mass. 364, 79 N.E. 745 (1907)

This case is found in two reporters: Massachusetts Reports and North Eastern Reporter. Hence, you can shepardize the case and obtain the same citing material from two different sets of Shepard's: **Shepard's Massachusetts Citations** and **Shepard's Northeastern Citations.**[74]

To shepardize a case means to obtain the following six kinds of information about the cited case (i.e., the case you are shepardizing):

1. The parallel cite of the case. The first entry in parenthesis is the parallel cite. See page 59 on the reasons why you may find no parallel cite.
2. The history of the case—all cases that are part of the same litigation, e.g., appeals, reversals.
3. Citing cases—other opinions that have mentioned or discussed the cited case, e.g., followed it, distinguished it or just mentioned it.
4. Citing legal periodical literature—articles or case notes which have analyzed or mentioned the cited case.
5. Citing annotations—annotations in ALR, ALR2d, ALR3d, ALR4th, ALR Fed that have analyzed or mentioned the cited case.
6. Citing opinion of the attorney general—an opinion of the attorney general that has analyzed or mentioned the cited case.

The great value of Shepard's as a case finder comes through items 3 to 5 above. They enable you to locate case law in addition to the cited case. If a citing case mentions or discusses the cited case, the two cases probably deal with similar facts and law. All citing cases, therefore, are potential leads to more case law on point for you. Similarly, a citing law review article or annotation will probably discuss a variety of cases in addition to the discussion of the cited case. Hence, again, you are led to more case law through Shepard's.

Items 2 and 3 above also enable you to do validation research.[75] They tell you if the cited case is still good law. Has it been reversed? Has it been discussed with approval by citing cases? Has it been ignored by other courts?

One final point before examining an excerpt from a Shepard's page. Recall that cases in reporters are broken down into headnotes at the beginning of the case.[76]   These headnotes are written either by the private publisher (such as West) or by the court clerk in official editions of the case.   Shepard's calls these headnotes of the case the "syllabus" of the case—small paragraph summaries of portions of the case found at the beginning of the case.   A case may consist of many issues, only a few of which may be relevant to your research problem.   The question then arises as to whether it is possible to narrow your shepardizing to those parts of the case which are most relevant to your research problem.   Yes.   It is possible to shepardize a portion of a case through its headnote or syllabus numbers.   In effect, you are shepardizing the headnote!   How is this done?

- The editors of Shepard's count the headnotes or syllabus paragraphs of the *cited* case.
- When the editors of Shepard's come across a *citing* case which deals with only one of the headnotes or syllabus paragraphs of the *cited* case, they indicate the number of the headnote or syllabi paragraph as part of the *citing* case in the columns of Shepard's.
- The number is printed as a small raised or elevated number—called a small superior figure—within the reference to the *citing* case.

Be careful.   It is easy to become confused.   The superior figure refers to the headnote or syllabi number of the *cited* case, not of the citing case.

For example, assume again that you are shepardizing Welch v. Swasey, 193 Mass. 364.   In the columns of Shepard's you find the following:

$$f193Mass.^8476$$

The *citing* case is 193 Mass. 476.   This case follows (agrees with) the *cited* case, Welch v. Swasey, 193 Mass. 364.   Note the raised number 8—the superior figure.   This 8 refers to the eighth headnote or syllabus of the *cited* case, Welch v. Swasey.   The *citing* case dealt with that portion of Welch which was summarized in the eighth headnote or syllabus of the Welch case.   Again, do not make the mistake of thinking that the small raised number refers to a headnote or syllabus in the citing case.   It refers to a headnote or syllabus number of the *cited* case.

We now look at a specimen page from Shepard's Massachusetts Citations (page 94) where we will begin to shepardize Welch v. Swasey, 193 Mass. 364. Read the oval inserts on this specimen page before carefully studying the comments that follow.

Let us assume that by legal research, you have located the case of Welch v. Swasey, reported in Volume 193 Massachusetts Reports at page 364.   This is the cited case which we want to shepardize.

The specimen page contains a reproduction of page 726 in the 1967 Case Edition of Shepard's Massachusetts Citations.   Note the number of the volume of reports "Vol. 193" in the upper left corner of the page.

An examination of the bold face type numbers appearing in the third column locates the page number "—364—".   This is the initial page of the case under consideration.   Following this page number you will find the citations "(79 NE 745)", "(118 AS 523)", "(23 Lns 1160)" indicating that the same case is also reported in 79 Northeastern Reporter 745, 118 American State Reports 523 and 23 Lawyers Reports Annotated, New Series 1160. These are parallel citations.

Assume you want to shepardize 193 Mass 364 (see third column)

SPECIMEN PAGE—Shepard's Massachusetts Citations. Case Edition, 1967

Vol. 193

MASSACHUSETTS REPORTS

317Mas²432	d283Mas³561	341Mas¹642	230Mas⁷190	**—392—**	219Mas¹506	264Mas²100	311Mas⁷370
326Mas²147	264Mas⁴607	269F²782	234Mas²602	(79NE739)	301Mas³327	270Mas¹173	'03-22EC64
184F¹220	297Mas³273	293F²406	234Mas⁴604	(9Lns695)	167F¹81	312Mas¹289	90AR755n
216F¹507	252F³516	324AR1316n	234Mas⁵609	201Mas¹540	534AR145n	320Mas¹626	55AR24n
248F²263	304Mas²642	155AR643n	241Mas¹528	237Mas²398	**—419—**	321Mas¹675	**—464—**
f258F¹299	d314Mas²682	41AR1304n	242Mas⁸32				(79NE784)
263F²1014	322Mas³219	**—351—**	f242Mas⁶34				295Mas³100
f39F²d540	322Mas⁸227	(79NE790)	245Mas8				242Mas¹534
6BUR234	328Mas³534	cc222F349	f250Mas560				250Mas¹457
8BUR151	d339Mas²728	203Mas²130	250Mas⁸71	280Mas¹330	f208Mas²566	(79NE797)	250Mas¹535
8BUR210	343Mas³779	203Mas²424	255Mas⁷171	210Mas¹552	(7Lns148)	319Mas¹308
11BUR142	182F⁴127	241Mas²474	257Mas¹153	**—400—**	213Mas¹294	197Mas³396	10BUR39
24MQ(1)2	245F2d³447	250Mas²314	264Mas¹87	(79NE774)	203Mas¹327	f236Mas¹223	202Mas²446	10BUR168
24MQ(4)9	50AR1366n	281Mas²166	270Mas¹524	217Mas¹32	256Mas²56	205Mas⁸171	35AR963n
59AR157n	**—336—**	343Mas¹371	286Mas¹618	244Mas¹306	257Mas¹50	208Mas⁸157	**—470—**
—324—	(79NE771)	343Mas²723	286Mas²618	250Mas¹87	262Mas¹580	215Mas²470	(79NE878)
(79NE734)	242Mas¹392	4BUR30	289Mas⁴185	256Mas¹153	319Mas²314	216Mas³180	247Mas¹203
196Mas483	282Mas376	39BUR494	315Mas⁷342	270Mas¹39	319Mas¹599	d216Mas214	333Mas¹777
d197Mas	101AR237n	40BUR228	323Mas¹650	284Mas¹9	326Mas¹460	217Mas³95	34AR49n
[¹178	**—339—**	78AR1040n	323Mas⁸650	308Mas¹405	335Mas²700	223Mas¹184	8AR965n
200Mas¹35	(79NE733)	45AR119n	324Mas¹⁰448	**—402—**	47ABA602	230Mas²391	**—479—**
206Mas²389	197Mas¹292	45AR143n	328Mas⁴676	(79NE776)	22AR578n	236Mas¹14	(79NE787)
207Mas¹501	d197Mas	45AR183n	333Mas⁴778	f195Mas¹128	114AR434n	d236Mas³538	**—482—**
d216Mas	[¹422	45AR250n	339Mas208				(79NE794)
[¹822	201Mas¹57	46AR160n	f41F2d¹938				284Mas¹521
216Mas²339	5AR815n	46AR191n	6AG182				339Mas¹710
220Mas¹30	**—341—**	46AR219n	6AG440				**—486—**
220Mas¹299	(79NE815)	46AR265n	7AG451	317Mas¹566	211Mas¹485	d263Mas¹75	(79NE763)
273Mas²29	(118AS516)	46AR385n	6BUR166				201Mas¹58
273Mas²476	(7Lns729)	**—356—**	6BUR306				204Mas337
326Mas¹795	f194Mas⁵459	(79NE742)	8BUR79				208Mas510
—327—	d195Mas	(9Lns874)	10BUR322		(79NE748)	321Mas¹73	205Mas¹461
(79NE818)	[¹318	202Mas¹495	10BUR324	74AR998n	202Mas²204	327Mas¹73	221Mas¹320
199Mas¹11	196Mas¹71	207Mas¹181	18BUR92	74AR1011n		341Mas¹699	308Mas¹545
202Mas⁴113	201Mas¹470	209Mas¹88	21BUR650				**—488—**
222Mas⁵261	205Mas¹3	214Mas²541	22BUR381				(80NE583)
268Mas⁴546	d205Mas²36	224Mas²360	37HLR842				cc191Mas441
292Mas⁴550	206Mas486	245Mas¹10	13MQ(6)72				c198Mas580
299Mas⁴3	207Mas¹498	265Mas³412	43MQ(3)61				194Mas573
299Mas⁵4	d207Mas	272Mas³220	48MQ(4)492				198Mas¹582
321Mas⁵108	[²563	295Mas²55	34AR46n				276Mas¹286
174F8³455	208Mas³447	339Mas²250	8AR965n				**—495—**
—331—	210Mas²456	266F²198	58AR1088n				(79NE738)
(79NE749)	212Mas²309	28F8²157	**—372—**				198Mas¹531
194Mas¹446	213Mas³329	46F8¹957	(79NE777)	315Mas³345	201Mas³265	46MQ(3)245	d203Mas¹261
199Mas¹541	f213Mas²597	46F8²958	233Mas¹253	319Mas²674	f202Mas³10	48MQ(3)318	204Mas¹201
220Mas¹581	f217Mas²421	41AR127n	324AR215n	7AG6	202Mas¹65	171AR369n	205Mas¹274
—332—	217Mas¹517	44AR1088n	**—383—**	42AR1467n	204Mas²229	**—453—**	229Mas¹44
(79NE765)	223Mas²494	126AR1095n	(79NE737)		209Mas349	(79NE775)	335Mas¹427
(7Lns1076)	d227Mas	126AR1097n	**—412—**			Mas¹555	345Mas¹41
196Mas²31	[²115	**—364—**				Mas³335	**—498—**
199Mas²448	d229Mas⁸67	(79NE745)				Mas¹286	(79NE796)
199Mas²475	f232Mas²551	(118AS523)				**—455—**	194Mas³575
201Mas²185	d233Mas	(23Lns1160)				(79NE770)	1MQ311
203Mas396	[²350	a214US91				212Mas²109	**—500—**
204Mas268	238Mas²231	a53LE923				227Mas²51	(79NE781)
206Mas⁸388	239Mas¹227	a29SC567				237Mas²507	201Mas²607
d207Mas⁸29	239Mas¹567	f193Mas⁸476	218Mas¹191	246Mas⁸389	206Mas³3	274Mas²501	205Mas⁴328
207Mas⁸448	244Mas²452	198Mas	260Mas¹385	285Mas³543	304Mas¹222	284Mas²506	210Mas280
217Mas⁸118	d245Mas	[¹¹256	260Mas¹397	305Mas⁴440	304Mas¹470	292Mas¹193	241Mas³544
220Mas⁸31	[¹122	200Mas¹484				300Mas²88	254Mas279
220Mas⁴32	d248Mas	d203Mas⁸29				309Mas²531	267Mas⁴101
224Mas⁸407	[²496	203Mas¹55				313Mas²416	304AR1164n
241Mas⁴79	d250Mas	206Mas¹432				337Mas²546	**—507—**
245Mas⁴121	[²245	f206Mas⁷433	312Mas¹645	**—415—**	**—444—**	6MQ(2)27	(79NE764)
246Mas⁸521	d251Mas259	208Mas¹622	337Mas⁷30	(79NE769)	(79NE821)	16MQ(5)218	195Mas⁴160
260Mas¹337	252Mas¹274	208Mas⁷630	f337Mas¹30	f196Mas²551	204Mas²354	**—458—**	196Mas⁴128
263Mas⁴218	d259Mas	219Mas	339Mas¹14	200Mas²193	208Mas²403	(79NE807)	196Mas²486
266Mas⁴543	[³328	[¹¹197	339Mas¹16	200Mas²343	224Mas¹584	216Mas⁷143	198Mas²571
267Mas³366	264Mas²368	220Mas¹275	4AG279	202Mas³224	h234Mas¹23	216Mas223	200Mas²543
f269Mas⁴63	297Mas¹195	222Mas	8AG474	204Mas¹481	d239Mas	222Mas⁵82	201Mas384
270Mas⁴266	303Mas¹244	[¹¹580	3AR1456n	205Mas²179	[¹232	236Mas¹347	f203Mas⁸5⁸4
276Mas⁴384	d316Mas²619	225Mas	23AR249n	205Mas¹370	h247Mas	240Mas⁷370	206Mas⁴545
277Mas⁴365	322Mas⁵294	[¹¹196	78AR825n	f212Mas³170	[¹213	256Mas⁷470	208Mas⁴118
279Mas⁴345	338Mas¹28	228Mas⁸374	86AR675n	216Mas⁸498	248Mas¹289	262Mas¹53	**Continued**

Circled annotations (in order):

- Followed with reference to paragraph six of syllabus
- Cited by lower federal court
- Cited in Boston University Law Review
- Cited in Harvard Law Review
- Cited in Massachusetts Law Quarterly
- Cited in annotations of Annotated Reports System
- Same case reported in Northeastern Reporter, American State Reports and Lawyers Reports Annotated, New Series
- Affirmed by United States Supreme Court
- Distinguished with reference to paragraph eight of syllabus

For later citations see any subsequent bound supplement or volume, the current issue of the periodically published paper-covered cumulative supplement and any current issue of the advance sheet

In obtaining the history of this case, you will observe that upon appeal to the United States Supreme Court it was affirmed "a" in 214 United States Reports "US" 91, 53 Lawyers' Edition, United States Supreme Court Reports "LE" 923 and 29 Supreme Court Reporter "SC" 567.

It is also to be observed by examining the abbreviations table at the beginning of the citator, that this case has been followed "f" and distinguished "d" in subsequent cases in the Massachusetts and federal courts.

In the citation "f242 Mas⁶ 34", the small superior figure "6" in advance of the citing page number 34 indicates that the principle of law brought out in the sixth paragraph of the syllabus (i.e., the headnotes) of 193 Mas 364 has been followed in 242 Mas 34.

In addition to the citations in point with paragraph six of the syllabus, note the numerous citations in point with other paragraphs of the syllabus of this case by the Massachusetts and federal courts. The cases dealing with a point of law in any particular paragraph of the syllabus may thus be referred to instantly without examining every citing case listed.

This case has also been cited in the Harvard Law Review "HLR", Boston University Law Review "BUR" and Massachusetts Law Quarterly "MQ".

The citations appearing in annotations of the Annotated Reports System are grouped together for convenience of use.

By examining this same volume and page number of the cited case in the other units of Shepard's Massachusetts Citations, all citations to this case will be found.

Shepard's Citations to cases will enable the researcher in a very short time to collect the entire body of case law that revolves around and about a cited case.

CHECKLIST #4a

CHECKLIST FOR SHEPARDIZING A CASE
1. You have a case you want to shepardize. In what reporter is this case found? Go to the set of Shepard's in the library that covers this reporter.
2. If the case you want to shepardize has a parallel cite which you already have, find out if the library has a set of Shepard's for the other reporter volumes in which the case is also found. You may be able to shepardize the case through more than one set of Shepard's. (There are sets of Shepard's for the individual state official reports and for all of the reporters of West's unofficial National Reporter System, supra p. 20.)
3. Go through the five steps to determine whether you have a complete set of Shepard's, supra p. 88. Read the box.
4. The general rule is that you must check the cite of the case you are shepardizing (the cited case) in *every* unit of a set of Shepard's. With experience you will learn, however, that it is possible to bypass some of the units of the set. There may be information on the front cover of one of the Shepard's volumes, for example, that will tell you that the reporter containing your cited case will not be covered in that Shepard's volume. You can bypass it and move on to other units mentioned in the box. It is recommended, however, that you not bypass anything early in your career. Wait until you feel very comfortable with Shepard's before bypassing anything.
5. Suppose that in one of the units of a set of Shepard's you find nothing listed for the cited case. This could mean one of three things:

CHECKLIST #4a—continued

CHECKLIST #4a—continued

(a) You are in the wrong set of Shepards.
(b) You are in the right set of Shepard's, but the Shepard's unit you are examining does not cover the particular volume of the reporter that contains your cited case. (See #4 above)
(c) You are in the right set of Shepard's. The silence in Shepard's about your cited case means that since the time of the printing of the last unit of Shepard's for that set, nothing has happened to the case—there is nothing for Shepard's to tell you.

6. Know the six kinds of information that you can obtain when shepardizing a case: parallel cites, history of cited case, citing cases, citing legal periodical literature, citing annotations, citing opinions of the attorney general.

7. The page number listed for every citing case is the page on which the cited case is mentioned. It is not the page on which the citing case begins.

8. Use the abbreviations tables and the Preface pages at the beginning of most units of Shepard's—and use them often.

9. A small "n" to the right of the page number of a citing case (e.g., 23 ALR 198n) means the cited case is found within an annotation (supra p. 83). A small "s" to the right of the page number of a citing case (e.g., 23 ALR 198s) means the cited case is found in a supplement to the annotation (supra p. 511).

10. Special care is needed in shepardizing a U.S. Supreme Court opinion in United States Shepard's, Case Edition. We have seen that there are three major cites to every opinion of the U.S. Supreme Court: U.S. (official), S.Ct. (West), L.Ed (Lawyers Co-op.). These are all parallel cites. In guideline #1 above, we said that cases with parallel cites can often be shepardized through more than one set of Shepard's. There is, however, only one set of Shepard's for U.S. Supreme Court opinions (United States Citations, Case Edition). The question arises as to whether you can shepardize the Supreme Court opinion through any one of the three cites. In the old days, the answer was no; you must shepardize through the U.S. cite. Today, you can shepardize through any of the three cites. It is recommended, however, that you shepardize *only* through the U.S. cite since you may pick up some citing material through the U.S. cite that is not available when you shepardize through the S.Ct. or L.Ed cites.

6. Shepardizing a Statute

You shepardize a statute in order to try to find the following seven kinds of information:

1. A parallel cite of the statute (found in parenthesis immediately after the section number of the statute). The parallel cite is to the *session law* edition of the statute (see discussion below).
2. The history of the statute in the legislature, e.g., amendments, new sections added, repealed, renumbered, etc.
3. The history of the statute in the courts, e.g., citing cases that have analyzed the statute, declared it constitutional, etc.
4. Citing administrative decisions, e.g., agency decisions that have analyzed the statute.

5. Citing legal periodical literature, e.g., law review articles that have analyzed the statute.

6. Citing annotations in ALR, ALR2d, ALR3d, ALR4th, ALR Fed that have analyzed the statute.

7. Citing opinions of the attorney general that have analyzed the statute.

When a statute is passed by the legislature, it comes out as a slip law and then in a form that may be called Session Laws, Laws, Acts, Acts and Resolves,[77] Statutes at Large,[78] etc.   (For convenience, all of the latter terms will be referred to below as the session law edition of the statutes.)   Session laws are arranged chronologically by years—the statutes are not arranged by subject matter in the session law volumes.   Finally, many of the session laws are put into statutory codes.[79]   They are *codified* which means that they *are* organized by subject matter rather than chronologically.

Most of the time you will be shepardizing a statute through its codified edition.[80]   The parallel cite will be to the session law edition of the statute. For example:

Codified Cite	**Session Law Cite**
Ohio Rev. Code Ann. § 45 (1978) ──────►	1975 Ohio Laws, C. 508
34 U.S.C. § 18(c) (1970) ──────────────►	87 Stat. 297 (1965)

Notice the totally different numbering system in the codified and session law cites—yet they are the same statutes.   Section 45 of the Ohio Revised Code Annotated is found word-for-word in Chapter (C.) 508 of the 1975 session laws of Ohio.   And section 18(c) of title 34 of the United States Code is found word-for-word in volume 87 of Statutes at Large (Stat.) on page 297.   Notice also the different years for the same statute.   The year in the session law cite is the year the legislature passed the statute.   The year in the codified cite, however, is usually the year of the codification which, as indicated above, comes later.

Shepard's has its own abbreviation system for citing session laws.   Suppose that you are shepardizing Kan.Stat.Ann. § 123 (1973)—a codified cite. Section 123 would be the cited statute—what you are shepardizing.   In the Shepard's columns for Kansas statutes, you might find:

> **Section 123**
> (1970C6)
> A1972C23
> Rp1975C45

The parallel cite in parenthesis is "1970C6" which means the 1970 Session Laws of the state of Kansas, Chapter 6.   The mention of a year in Shepard's for statutes usually means the sessions laws for that year.   (You would find out the meaning of "C" by checking the abbreviations tables at the beginning of the Shepard's volume.)

Immediately beneath the parenthesis in the above example you find two other references to session laws:

A1972C23→In the 1972 Session Laws of Kansas, Chapter 23, there was an amendment to section 123 (which is what "A" means according to Shepard's abbreviation tables)

Rp1975C45→In the 1975 Session Laws of Kansas, Chapter 45, section 123 was repealed in part (which is what "Rp" means according to Shepard's abbreviation tables).

You will note that Shepard's does *not* tell you what the amendment was, nor what was repealed in part. How do you find this out? Two ways. First, you go to the session laws if your library has them. Second, you go to the cited statute (§ 123) in the codified code (here the Kansas Statutes Annotated). At the bottom of the statute in the code, there may be a legislative history note which will summarize amendments, repeals, etc. (Also check this same note for the cited statute in the pocket part of the code volume you are using.)

Other citing material given in Shepard's for a statute is less complicated. For example, there are cites to citing cases, citing law review articles, etc. that follow a very similar pattern to the citing material for cases you are shepardizing.[81]

The biggest headache in shepardizing a statute is due to the fact that statutory codes often come out in new editions with renumbered sections. Section 45 on hunting licenses, for example, may now be section 14(b) in a new edition of the code. Furthermore, the two sections may also be in totally different titles of the code. The basic rule is that you shepardize a statute through its *current* code edition. Hence, you would shepardize the hunting statute above through section 14(b) of its present title.

Suppose, however, that you do not know the current cite of a statute. You may be reading an old case or law review article which cites a statute by its old number. How do you shepardize such a statute? You must first locate its current cite. First go to the current edition of the statutory code. You will not be able to find the statute under the old cite because of the renumbering. Look for *transfer tables* [82] somewhere in the current statutory code, e.g., at the beginning of the first volume of the statutory code, at the beginning of those volumes of the statutory code that deal with the general subject matter of the statute (if you know the general subject matter), at the beginning of the General Index volumes of the statutory code, in special pamphlets at the end of the statutory code, etc. Use these transfer tables to find out what the *current* citation of your statute is. Then go to Shepard's and shepardize the statute under its current cite.

Assume that you want to shepardize a federal statute—in the U.S. Code (the statutory cite in USCA and USCA is the same as in USC [83]). As with the shepardizing of every statute, you must shepardize through the most current edition of the code. A new edition of the USC comes out every six years, e.g., 1970 Edition, 1976 Edition, 1982 Edition. In between editions, the USC is supplemented by annual Supplement volumes, e.g., Supplement 1977 (I), Supplement 1978 (II). Shepardize your statute through the latest code edition *and* through any of the Supplement years indicated on the top of the Shepard's pages used to shepardize a federal statute—Shepard's United States Citations, Statute Edition.[84]

Assume that the most current code edition is the 1970 edition.   You want to shepardize 18 USC § 700 (1970).   You trace this cite through all of the units of Shepard's United States Citations, Statute Edition.   The following is an excerpt from a page in one of these units:

United
States
Code, 1970
Edition
and
Supple-
ment, 1972

TITLE 18

§ 700
Ad82St291   1
C302FS1112   2

394U'S604
22LE502
89SC1372
445F2d226
462F2d96
479F2d1177   3
313FS49
317FS138
322FS593
324FS1278
343FS165
414S504n   5

Subsec. a
C454F2d972
C462F2d96
445F2d226
479F2d1179
324FS1278

Subsec. b   6
C462F2d96
445F2d226

Subsec. c
394US508
22LE588
89SC1360
322FS585

UNITED STATES CODE
(*Illustrative Statute*)

Citations to section "§" 700 of Title 18 of the United States Code, 1970 Edition and Supplement 2, 1972 are shown in the left margin of this page.   In Shepard's United States Citations, Statute Edition any citation to a section of the United States Code presently in effect is shown as is illustrated here and any citation to a section of the United States Code no longer in effect is shown as referring to the section number of the United States Code of the year when that section number last appeared.

Citations to each cited statutory provision are grouped as follows:

1. amendments, repeals, etc. by acts of Congress subsequent to 1962;
2. citations by the United States Supreme Court and the lower federal courts analyzed as to constitutionality or validity;
3. other citations by the United States Supreme Court and the lower federal courts;
4. citations in articles in the American Bar Association Journal;
5. citations in annotations of the Lawyers' Edition, United States Supreme Court Reports and of the American Law Reports;
6. citations to specific subdivisions of the statute.

For the purpose of illustration only, this grouping has been indicated by bracketing the citations accordingly.   It will be noted that as yet there are no citations in group four.

The first citation shown indicates that section 700 of Title 18 was added "Ad" by an act of Congress printed in 82 United States Statutes at Large "St" at page 291.   The section is next shown to have been held constitutional "C" by a lower federal court in a case reported in 302 Federal Supplement "FS" 1112 and to have been cited without particular comment in several cases before the federal courts and the United States Supreme Court.   The section was also cited in an annotation "n" of the American Law Reports, Third Series "A^3 ".

Citing references to specific subdivisions of the section are then shown.   Subsection "Subsec." a of section 700 was held constitutional in two lower federal court cases reported in 454 F2d 972 and 462 F2d 96.

CHECKLIST #4b

CHECKLIST FOR SHEPARDIZING A STATUTE
1. Go to the set of Shepard's that will enable you to shepardize your statute. For federal statutes, it is Shepard's United States Citations, Statute Edition.   For state statutes, go to the set of Shepard's for your state.   The same set of Shepard's may cover both state cases and statutes in the same units or in different case and statute editions of the set.
2. You must have the codified cite of the statute in its latest edition of the statutory code.   If your cite is to an earlier edition of the code, try to find the cite to the current code through transfer tables within the latest statutory code itself.

CHECKLIST #4b—continued

CHECKLIST #4b—continued

3. If the only cite you have is a session law cite of the statute (e.g., Laws, Statutes at Large) you can shepardize the statute only if the session law was never codified by the legislature. If the session law was codified, you must translate the session law cite into its codified cite in order to shepardize it. For federal statutes, the session laws are in Statutes at Large (Stat. or St.). To translate a Stat. cite into a U.S.C. cite, check Table III in the Tables volume of U.S.C., or of U.S.C.A., or of U.S.C.S. Table 2 in U.S. Code Congressional and Administrative News, supra p. 48 and infra p. 129, will also enable you to translate a Stat. cite into a U.S.C. cite. To translate a state session law cite into the codified cite, look for transfer tables within the current statutory code.

4. Go through the five steps to determine whether you have a complete set of Shephard's, supra p. 88. Read the box.

5. Check your cite in *every* unit of Shepard's. It is recommended that you work backwards so that you obtain the latest citing material first.

6. At the top of a Shepard's page, and in its columns, look for your statute by the name of the code, year, article, chapter, title, section—according to how the statute is identified in its cite. Repeat this for every unit of Shepard's.

7. Know the seven kinds of information you can obtain by shepardizing a statute: parallel cite (not always given), history of the statute in the legislature, history of the statute in the courts, citing administrative decisions, citing legal periodical literature, citing annotations, citing opinions of the attorney general.

8. The history of the statute in the legislature will give you the citing material in session law form, e.g., A 1980 C 45. This refers to the 1980 Laws of the legislature, chapter 45. Another example; A 34 St. 654. This refers to volume 34, page 654 of the Statutes at Large. If you want to locate these session laws, find out if your library keeps the session laws. Also, check the legislative history reference after the statute in the statutory code.

9. Watch for the following notation in the columns of Shepard's: "et seq." It means, "and following." The citing material may be analyzing more than one statutory section. You should check the citing material that follows an "et seq." notation. Your specific statute may be covered by the discussion in the citing material.

10. Use the abbreviation tables and the Preface material at the beginning of most of the units of the set of Shepard's. And use them often.

11. If your state code has gone through revisions or renumberings, read the early pages in the statutory code to try to obtain an explanation of what has happened. This information may be of considerable help to you in interpreting the data provided in the Shepard's units for your state code.

7. *Shepardizing a Regulation*

You cannot shepardize regulations of state agencies. No sets of Shepard's cover state regulations. Until recently, the same was true of federal regulations. Today, however, it is possible to shepardize federal regulations in the Code of Federal Regulations (C.F.R.). This is done through Shepard's Code of Federal Regulations Citations.[85] (It will also allow you to shepardize executive orders and reorganization plans.)

The C.F.R. comes out in new edition every year.[86]   (See example on page 102.)   All the changes that have occurred during the year are incorporated in the new yearly edition.   Two kinds of changes can be made:

1. those changes made by the agency itself, e.g., amendments, repeals, renumbering—this is the history of the regulation in the agency
2. those changes forced on the agency by the courts, e.g., declaring the regulation invalid—this is the history of the regulation in the courts

Unfortunately, Shepard's will only give you the history of the regulation *in the courts* (plus commentary on the regulation in legal periodical literature and in annotations).   The columns of Shepard's will *not* give you the history of the regulation in the agency.   (To obtain the latter, you must check elsewhere, e.g., the "Sections Affected" tables in the Federal Register.[87])   The main value of the Shepard's for C.F.R is that it will tell you what *the courts* have said about the regulation (plus the periodical and annotation commentary.)

When shepardizing through the Shepard's C.F.R. Citations, the cited material, of course, is the federal regulation—referred to below as the cited regulation.   There are two kinds of *citing* material provided by Shepard's:

1. Citing cases, periodicals and annotations that refer to the cited regulation by year, i.e., by edition
2. Citing cases, periodicals and annotations that refer to the cited regulation without specifying the year or edition of the regulation.

For the first kind of citing material, Shepard's gives you a small elevated asterisk just before a given year.   If, for example, you were shepardizing 12 C.F.R. § 218.111(j), you might find the following:

§ 218.111 (j)
420F2d90 *1965

The citing material is a citing case—420 F.2d 90.   The small asterisk means that the citing case discussed section 218.111(j) and this case specifically identified the year of this regulation—1965.   This year is *not* the year of the citing case.   It is the year of the cited regulation.

Now let us examine the second kind of citing material mentioned above. There may be citing material that mentions the regulation, but does not tell us the specific year or edition of that regulation.   Shepard's uses an elevated triangle in such situations.   If, for example, you were shepardizing 12 C.F.R. § 9.18(a)(3), you might find the following:

§ 9.18 (a) (3)
274FS628 △1967

The citing material is a citing case—274 F.Supp. 628.   The small triangle means that the citing case discussed section 9.18(a)(3) but did not refer to the year or edition of section 9.18(a)(3).   The year 1967 is the year of the citing case and not the year of the cited regulation.   The citing case in 274 F.Supp. 628 was decided in 1967.

CODE OF FEDERAL REGULATIONS

CFR
TITLE
42

§53.111
323F2d965 △1963
458F2d1117 △1972
551F2d333 *1972
Va559F2d973 △1977
327FS113 △1971
359FS911 *1973
Vp373FS551 △1974
373FS559 △1974
409FS711 △1976
Up453FS410 *1973
453FS680 *1976
    Mass
382NE1043 *1977
    NY
413S2d88 △1979
    Ore
582P2d48 *1976
88YLJ277 *1977
11ALRF684n △1972

Shepard's Code of Federal Regulations Citations shows citations to the Code of Federal Regulations and to Presidential Proclamations, Executive Orders and Reorganization Plans as cited by the United States Supreme Court, by the lower federal courts and by state courts in cases reported in any unit of the National Reporter System, in annotations of Lawyers' Edition, United States Supreme Court Reports and American Law Reports. In addition, citations appearing in articles in selected leading law reviews and in the American Bar Association Journal are shown.

Because of frequent revisions of the Code of Federal Regulations, a year is shown with each citation reference as an indication of its currentness.

If the citing source refers to the date of the cited CFR rule or regulation, the cited year is shown, preceded by the symbol *. If a rule or regulation is cited without a CFR date, the year of the citing reference is shown, preceded by the symbol △. By noting the year included in each citation reference, the user can then determine if citations are to current or superseded provisions of the Code of Federal Regulations.

Citations to each provision of the Code of Federal Regulations are grouped as follows:

1. citations by the United States Supreme Court and the lower federal courts analyzed as to constitutionality or validity;

2. citations by state court cases reported in the National Reporter System arranged alphabetically by the abbreviation for the state to which they pertain;

3. citations in articles in selected law reviews and in the American Bar Association Journal; and

4. citations in annotations in Lawyers' Edition; United States Supreme Court Reports and in the American Law Reports.

Letter abbreviations indicate holdings by the courts as to constitutionality or validity. The 1973 version of section 53.111 was held unconstitutional in part "Up" by a United States District Court case reported in 453 Federal Supplement "FS" 410. Previously, another United States District Court decision had held §53.111 void or invalid in part "Vp". Subsequently, the United States Court of Appeals in 1977 determined that §53.111 was valid.

Section 53.111 has also been cited by the Courts of Massachusetts, New York and Oregon. A law review citation is shown by the reference 88 Yale Law Journal "YLJ" 277, and a citation in an annotation "n" is shown by the reference 11 American Law Reports, Federal "ALRF" 1972.

CHECKLIST #4c

CHECKLIST FOR SHEPARDIZING A FEDERAL REGULATION
1. Obtain the correct set of Shepard's Code of Federal Regulations Citations. The regulation you want to shepardize must appear in the C.F.R.
2. Follow the five steps to determine whether you have a complete set of Shepard's for this set.   Read the box.   (Supra p. 88)
3. Shepardize your regulation through every unit of this set of Shepard's.
4. This set of Shepard's will give you two kinds of information: (a) Citing material that analyzes a regulation of a specific year or edition (indicated by asterisk next to the year of the regulation) (b) Citing material that analyzes a regulation without referring to the specific year or edition of the regulation (indicated by triangle next to the year of the citing material)

CHECKLIST #4c—continued

CHECKLIST #4c—continued

The citing material includes citing cases, citing legal periodical literature and citing annotations.
5. This set of Shepard's does not directly tell you what amendments, revisions or other changes were made by the agencies in the regulations.   You are only told what the courts have said about the regulations.   (To find out what the agencies have done to the regulations, you must check the "Sections Affected" tables in the Federal Register, and the LSA pamphlet. (Infra p. 138.)
6. Check the abbreviations and Preface at the beginning of most of the Shepard's units.   Use them often.
7. All regulations in C.F.R. are based on statutes of Congress.   You can find out what statutes in U.S.C. are the authority for particular regulations in C.F.R. by checking the "authority" reference under many of the regulations in C.F.R.   Once you know the statute which is the basis for the regulation, you might want to shepardize that statute for more law in the area. (See Checklist 4b above on shepardizing a statute.)

5.   LOOSE LEAF SERVICES

Loose leaf services are law books with a three ring or post binder structure.[88] Additions to these services are made frequently, e.g., monthly or sooner. The main publishers of these services are Bureau of National Affairs (BNA), Commerce Clearing House (CCH), Prentice Hall (PH) and Matthew Bender.[89] They cover numerous broad areas of the law, e.g., criminal law, taxes, corporate law, unions, etc.   You should assume that one or more loose leaf services exist for the topic of your research problem until you prove to yourself otherwise.   Benefits provided by the loose leaf services often include:

- recent court opinion and/or summaries of opinions
- relevant legislation—usually explained in some detail
- administrative regulations and decisions and/or summaries of them (some of this material may not be available elsewhere)
- references to relevant studies and reports
- practice tips

In short, the loose leaf services are extremely valuable.

Unfortunately, however, they are sometimes awkward to use.   Not uncommonly, library staff and/or students have misfiled some of the updating pages and/or library users of the loose leaf services misfile pages that they take out for xeroxing or other photocopying.

There is no standard order to the loose leaf books.   You may find, for example:

- different colored pages to indicate more recent material
- indexes at the end of the books, in the middle, in the beginning
- summaries, summaries of summaries
- organization by page number, organization by section number, organization by paragraph number, combination of the above
- one volume, multi volumes of the same loose leaf service
- bound volumes that accompany the three ring or post volumes
- transfer binders that contain current material
- etc.

You must approach each loose leaf service as a puzzle that is sitting on the shelf waiting for you to figure out its structure.

CHECKLIST #5

CHECKLIST FOR FINDING AND USING LOOSE LEAF SERVICES
1. Divide your research problem into its major topics, e.g., family law, tax law, anti-trust law, etc.   Assume that one or more loose leaf services exist for these topics until you have demonstrated to yourself otherwise.
2. Find out where in your library the loose leaf services are located.   Are they all together?   Are they located in certain subject areas?
3. Check the card catalog.   (See Checklist #1 supra p. 78.)   Use the CARTWHEEL to help you use the catalog.   Check subject heading cards for your topics to see if loose leaf services are mentioned.   Check the names of the major publishers of loose leaf services, e.g., Bureau of National Affairs, Commerce Clearing House, Prentice Hall, Matthew Bender, etc.
4. Ask your librarian if s/he knows of loose leaf services on the major topics of your research.
5. Call other law libraries in your area (supra p. 8).   Ask the librarians there if they know of loose leaf services on the major topics of your research.   See if they can identify loose leaf services that you could not identify through your own library.
6. Speak to experts in the area of the law, e.g., professors.   (See Checklist #9, infra p. 110).   Ask them about loose leaf services.
7. Once you have a loose leaf service in front of you, you must figure out how to use it: (a) Read any preface or explanation material in the front of the volumes of the loose leaf service (b) Ask the librarian if s/he can give you some help using it (c) Ask a teacher who is an expert in the area if s/he can give you a brief demonstration on its use (d) Ask a fellow student whom you know is familiar with the service (e) Read any pamphlets or promotional literature put out by the publishers on using the loose leaf services (supra p. 103) (f) Do the best that you can to struggle through the set on your own For each loose leaf service you need to know: • what it contains/what it does not contain • how it is indexed • how it is supplemented • what its special features are • how many volumes or units it has and the interrelationship among them You obtain this information through techniques (a) to (f) above.
8. In your research memo, you rarely cite the loose leaf service unless the material you found there does not exist elsewhere.   Use the loose leaf service mainly as background research (supra p. 75) and as a search tool to find cases, statutes, regulations, etc., i.e., to find primary authority (supra p. 50).

6. LEGAL PERIODICAL LITERATURE

Legal periodical literature [90] consists of:

• lead articles written by individuals who have extensively researched a topic

- case notes which summarize and comment upon recent important court opinions
- book reviews

Most periodicals are published by law students who are "on law review" at their law school.   (Such periodicals are often called law reviews or law journals.)   There are hundreds of legal periodicals containing a wealth of information for the researcher.

The big question is: how can you locate legal periodical literature on point?   Is there an index to the hundreds of periodicals and to the tens of thousands of articles, case notes and other material in them?   Three index systems exist:

- Index to Legal Periodicals (ILP)
- Current Law Index (CLI)
- Legal Resource Index (LRI)

LRI is more comprehensive than CLI and ILP; CLI is more comprehensive than ILP.   Comprehensiveness is determined by the number of periodicals indexed.   The benefit of a comprehensive index is that you obtain access to more periodicals; Unfortunately, most law libraries will not have all the periodicals mentioned in the index.   You may be obtaining cites to periodicals that your library does not have.   For such periodicals that you need, you will have to check other libraries in the area.[91]

(1)   Features of Index to Legal Periodicals (ILP):

- The ILP first comes out in pamphlets which are later cumulated into bound yearly volumes
- You must check each ILP pamphlet and each ILP bound volume for whatever years you want
- ILP regularly adds new periodicals to be indexed
- Every ILP pamphlet and bound volume has several sections:
    (i) a subject-and-author index
    (ii) a table of cases commented on
    (iii) a book review index
    (iv) a table of statutes commented on (added recently)
- There are abbreviations tables at the beginning of every pamphlet and bound volume
- The "subject" portion of the subject and author index is easy to use; you are led directly to the cites of periodical literature under the subjects relevant to your research topics
- The "author" portion of the subject-and-author index is more complex; if you know the name of an author but not the title of his/her article, you look for that author's name in the subject-and-author index; under his/her name you will find one or more topics and capital letters in parenthesis after the topics; go to those topics in the subject-and-author-index; under those topics, look for articles beginning with the capital letters you found in parenthesis initially until you locate the article by the author you want
- Toward the end of every pamphlet and bound volume there is a Table of Cases Commented On; suppose that elsewhere in your research you have come across an important case; you now want to know if that case was ever

commented upon (i.e., noted) in the legal periodicals; go to the ILP pamphlet or bound volume that covers the year of the case and check the Table of Cases Commented On

- The Table of Statutes Commented on will tell you where you can find periodical literature analyzing certain statutes
- At the end of every pamphlet and bound volume there is a book review index if you are looking for a book review of a law book (particularly a treatise [92]) you have come across elsewhere in your research; go to the ILP pamphlet or bound volume that covers the year of publication of the book on which you are seeking book reviews

(2)   Features of Current Law Index (CLI):

- The CLI first comes out in monthly pamphlets which are later cumulated into quarterly and annual issues
- CLI indexes more periodical literature than ILP
- CLI regularly adds new periodicals to be indexed
- Check all monthly pamphlets since the last quarterly pamphlet; check all quarterly pamphlets, check all annual issues for the years you want
- There are four indexes within each CLI unit
  (i) a subject index
  (ii) an author-title index
  (iii) a table of cases
  (iv) a table of statutes

- There are abbreviations tables at the beginning of every CLI unit
- The subject index gives full citations to periodicals under topic and under author's name
- The table of cases is valuable if you already know the name of a case located elsewhere in your research; to find out if that case was commented upon, check the table of cases in the CLI unit that covers the year of the case (this table of cases feature is similar to the "table of cases commented on" in ILP)
- the table of statutes is equally valuable; if you already have the name of a statute from your other research, look for the name of that statute in the table of statutes for the CLI unit that covers the approximate time the statute was passed (e.g., Atomic Energy Act; California Fair Employment Practices Act)
- The CLI is relatively new; hence, expect to find additional features to be added in the future

(3)   Features of Legal Resource Index (LRI):

- LRI comes out in microfilm to be used with a special viewer machine, some of which have coin-operated copiers (see illustration on page 107).
- LRI indexes more periodical literature than ILP or CLI
- LRI regularly adds new material to be indexed each year
- Each microfilm covers a five year period
- The indexes within LRI are similar to those described above for CLI (LRI and CLI are published by the same company—Information Access Corp.)
- The LRI is relatively new; hence, expect to find additional features in the future (printed annual volumes, online searchable data base facilities, etc.)

NOTE ON OTHER INDEX SYSTEMS

A number of other index systems exist:

- Jones-Chipman Index to Legal Periodical Literature
  (covering periodical literature up to 1937 only)
- Index to Periodical Articles Related to Law
  (covers periodicals not listed in ILP; this Index to Periodical Articles Related to Law is less needed today because of the recent publication of CLI and LRI which are also more comprehensive than ILP)
- Index to Foreign Legal Periodicals
  (covers periodicals many of which are also indexed in ILP, CLI and LRI)
- Index to Canadian Legal Periodical Literature
- Index Medicus
  (covers medical periodicals—available in medical libraries)
- Medline
  (a computer search system for medical periodicals—available in medical libraries)

CHECKLIST #6

CHECKLIST FOR FINDING LEGAL PERIODICAL LITERATURE
1. You must include a search for legal periodical literature as background research (supra p. 76) and for leads to primary authority (supra. p. 50) particularly through the extensive footnotes of legal periodical literature. Scholarly articles can be cited in your research memo.
2. There are three major index systems: Index to Legal Periodicals (ILP), Current Law Index (CLI) and Legal Resource Index (LRI).
3. Use all three of the major index systems in your legal research. The CARTWHEEL will help you locate material in them (supra p. 70).

CHECKLIST #6—continued

CHECKLIST #6—continued

4. Within ILP there are separate indexes; within CLI there are separate indexes; within LRI there are separate indexes; you should become familiar with all of these internal index features (supra p. 105).
5. Start with the subject headings index within ILP, CLI and LRI.
6. Identify the name and date of every important case that you have found in your research thus far.   Go to the table of cases in ILP and in CLI and in LRI to find out if there is any periodical literature that has commented on that case.   (Go to the ILP, CLI and LRI units that would cover the year the case was decided.   To be safe, also check their units for two years after the date of the case.)
7. If you are researching a statute, find out if there is any periodical literature that has commented on the statute.   This is done in two ways: (a) check the table of statutes in CLI, LRI, and ILP (b) break your statute down into its major topics; check these topics in the subject indexes of IPL, CLI and LRI to see if any periodical literature has been written on them.
8. If you know the name of an author who is well known for writing on a particular topic, you can also check for periodical literature written by that author under his/her name in ILP, CLI, and LRI.
9. Ask your librarian if the library has any other indexes to legal periodical literature, particularly in specialty areas of the law.
10. It is possible to shepardize legal periodical literature.   (Supra p. 45)   If you want to know whether the periodical article, note or comment was ever mentioned in a court opinion, go to Shepard's Law Review Citations.

7. LEGAL ENCYCLOPEDIAS

Here our main concern is using the major national encyclopedias: American Jurisprudence 2d (Am Jur 2d) and Corpus Juris Secundum.   We will not discuss the smaller encyclopedias that cover the law of individual states.[93]

CHECKLIST # 7

CHECKLIST FOR USING LEGAL ENCYCLOPEDIAS
1. Use both Am Jur 2d and CJS for the following purposes: (a) As background research for areas of the law that are new to you (supra p. 76) (b) For leads to primary authority, e.g., cases, statutes, etc.

CHECKLIST #7—continued

CHECKLIST #7—continued

> 2. Both legal encyclopedias have multi-volume general indexes at the end of their sets.   Use the CARTWHEEL to help you locate material in them (supra p. 70).   In addition to these general indexes, Am Jur 2d has an index to each volume and CJS has an index for each of the topics or titles covered.   Use the CARTWHEEL for these indexes as well.

> 3. Both Am Jur 2d and CJS have extensive footnotes for leads to primary authority.

> 4. Both Am Jur 2d and CJS are supplemented by pocket parts and by revisions of individual volumes.

> 5. There is no table of cases in either Am Jur 2d or CJS.

> 6. There is no table of statutes in CJS.   In Am Jur 2d, however, there is a separate volume called Table of Statutes and Rules Cited.   Check this Table if from your other research you have found a relevant statute which you want to find discussed in Am Jur 2d.

> 7. Am Jur 2d is published by Lawyers Co-op.   CJS is published by West. Within these legal encyclopedias, the publishers try to cross-reference you to other research books that they publish.   In Am Jur 2d, for example, Lawyers Co-op will refer you to annotations in ALR, ALR 2d, ALR 3d, ALR 4th, and ALR Fed.   (See Checklist #3 on finding and updating these annotations, supra p. 86).   In CJS, West will refer you to its key number digests.   (See Checklist #2 on using the digests of West, supra p. 81.)

> 8. Find out if your library has a local encyclopedia that is limited to the law of your state.

8.   TREATISES

A treatise is any book written by private individuals on a topic of law.[94]   Falling into the category of treatises are hornbooks, handbooks, and formbooks. There are single-volume treatises such as Prosser on Torts, as well as multi-volume treatises such as Am Jur Legal Forms, Am Jur Proof of Facts, Am Jur Pleading and Practice Forms, Am Jur Trials, Moore's Federal Practice, Collier on Bankruptcy, etc.

Since treatises try to give explanations of the law and references to primary authority, they are similar to legal encyclopedias, [95] legal periodical literature,[96] annotations [97] and loose leaf services.[98].

CHECKLIST #8

CHECKLIST FOR FINDING AND USING TREATISES
1.   Always look for treatises on the topics of your research problem.   Assume that three or four such treatises exist and are relevant to your problem until you prove to yourself otherwise.
2.   Treatises are useful as background research (supra p. 76), and as leads to primary authority (supra p. 50).   Scholarly treatises can also be cited in your research memo.
3.   Many treatises are updated by pocket parts, supplemental volumes, and page inserts if the treatise has a three ring or post binding structure.

CHECKLIST #8—continued

CHECKLIST #8—continued

---

4. Start your search for treatises in the card catalog using the CARTWHEEL as a guide (supra p. 70). See Checklist #1 on using the catalog (supra p. 78).

---

5. Check with experts in the area of law in which you are interested, e.g., teachers, for recommendations on treatises you should check.

---

6. If your library has open stacks, find the treatise section (e.g., with KF call numbers). Locate the areas where treatises on your topic are covered. (The card catalog will give you leads to such areas by the call numbers of books on the topic.) Browse through the shelves in these areas of the stacks to try to find additional treatises. (Some treatises, however, may be on reserve.)

---

7. Once you have found a treatise, check that author's name in the Index to Legal Periodicals (ILP), the Current Law Index (CLI) and in the Legal Resource Index (LRI) to try to find periodical literature on the topic by the same author. (See Checklist #6 on finding legal periodical literature, supra p. 107).

---

9. PHONE AND MAIL—SPEAK TO THE EXPERTS

Don't be reluctant to call or write recognized experts on the topics of your research. You can ask for leads to important cases, regulations, treatises, legal periodical literature, leads to other experts, leads to current or recent litigation, etc. Sometimes you can even discuss the facts of your research to obtain their perception of your direction. The worst that can happen is that they will ignore your request or simply say no. You will find, however, that many experts are quite willing to help you free of charge, so long as you are respectful and do not give the impression that you want more than a few moments of their time. You do not ask to come over to spend an afternoon!

CHECKLIST #9

CHECKLIST FOR DOING PHONE AND MAIL RESEARCH
1. Your goal is someone who is an expert in the area of your research problem. You want to write this person or talk to him/her briefly on the phone. It is usually not wise for you to try to go see the expert (unless s/he is on the faculty of your school).
2. Do not try to contact an expert until you have done a substantial amount of research on your own first, e.g., you should have already checked the major cases, statutes, regulations, treatises, legal periodical literature, annotations, etc.
3. Jot down the questions you want to ask the expert. Make the questions short and to the point. For example, "Do you know of any recent case law on the liability of a municipality for . . . ?" "Could you give me any leads to literature on the doctrine of promissory estoppel as it applies to . . . ?" "Do you know anyone who has done any research on the new EPA regulations whom I could contact?" "Do you know of anyone currently litigating section 307?" Do *not* recite all the facts of the research problem to the expert and say, "What should I do?" If the expert wants more facts from you, let him/her ask you for them. You must create the impression that you want no more than a few seconds of the expert's time. If they want to give your request more attention, they will let you know by continuing the conversation or by writing you a longer letter.

CHECKLIST #9—continued

CHECKLIST #9—continued

4. Introduce yourself as someone doing research on a problem, e.g., as a student.   State how you got their name (see guidelines below) and then state how grateful you would be if you could ask them a "quick question."

5. Your introductory comments should state how you came across their name and learned of their expertise, e.g., "I read your law review article on . . . ."   "I saw your name as an attorney of record in the case of . . . reported in . . . ."   "Mr/Ms . . . told me you were an expert in this area and recommended that I contact you."

6. Calling is always preferable to using the mail, unless calling is impractical because of distance.

7. Where do you find these experts?   A number of possibilities exist:
   (a) *Special interest groups and associations.*
      Contact lawyers within these groups and associations, e.g., unions, environmental groups, business associations.   Ask your librarian for lists of such groups and associations, e.g., the Encyclopedia of Associations, the Directory of Directories.
   (b) *Government agencies.*
      Contact the law department of the agencies that have something to do with the topics of your research problem.   (The CARTWHEEL should help you think of these agencies, supra p. 70.)
   (c) *Specialty libraries.*
      Ask your librarian for lists of libraries, e.g., Directory of Special Libraries and Information Centers.   (Supra p. 8)
   (d) *Law Professors*
      Check, of course, your own school.   Also, ask your librarian if the library has the AALS Law Teachers Directory which lists teachers by name and specialty.
   (e) *Attorneys of record*
      If you have found a recent court opinion on point, the names of the attorneys for the case are printed at the beginning of the opinion. You can obtain the addresses of the attorneys in Martindale-Hubbell Law Directory (supra p. 39).   These attorneys may be willing to send you a copy of appellate briefs on the case.   Also try to find out about on-going litigation in the courts.   Often you are permitted to go to the court clerk's office and examine pleadings, appellate briefs, etc. Finally, don't forget to check the closed case files of your own office for prior research that has already been done in the same area as your problem.
   (f) *Authors of legal periodical literature and of treatises.*
      Obtain the address of the author from Martindale-Hubbell Law Directory, by checking the Law Teachers Directory, or by contacting the publisher of the legal periodical or treatise (supra p. 5).   If you write to the publisher, it may be wise for you to enclose the letter you want to send to the author and ask the publisher to forward it to the author.

8. Be concerned about ethics and conflict of interest.   If your research is on a real case, you cannot contact an expert who happens to work for the other side!

10.   COMPUTERS

If you have access to any of the computers, use them.   The cost of using such computers can be extremely high (e.g., over $100 per hour).   You will need a demonstration on how to operate the computer from the librarian in charge or from the company that produces the computer. The major computers are listed below.

(a) WESTLAW by West Publishing Company

WESTLAW stores headnotes and full text opinions of the National Reporter System, the United States Code, U.S. Supreme Court opinions, U.S. Court of Appeals opinions, U.S. District Court opinions, Code of Federal Regulations, Shepard's Citations, the Forensic Services Directory, and more. Each day more material is added to WESTLAW.

(b) LEXIS by Mead Data Central, Inc.

LEXIS stores the full text of a number of legal documents, e.g., the United States Code, U.S. Supreme Court opinions, decisions of the Federal Trade Commission, the Securities and Exchange Commission, Congressional reports, many state court opinions, etc. As with WESTLAW, more material is being added regularly.

(c) Auto-Cite by Lawyers Co-operative Company

Auto-Cite permits you to check the accuracy of a legal citation. The Auto-Cite computer also give parallel cites and cites to other opinions in the same litigation.

(d) JURIS by the U.S. Department of Justice

JURIS is a computer that enables you to find case law. It is now available only to Justice Department employees.

(e) FLITE by the U.S. Department of Defense (Air Force)

FLITE is a computer that enables you to locate federal statutes, some federal court opinions, military law materials, etc. Available only to federal employees.

Section O.   READING AND FINDING CASE LAW

In this section we will first look at the structure of a court opinion and discuss how it is read. Then we will focus on the techniques of finding case law which will draw on the material discussed thus far in the Chapter.

READING CASE LAW

The following is an opinion printed in full from one of the reporters—the California Reporter. The circled numbers are explained after the opinion.

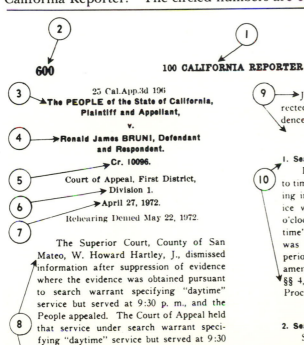

and 10 o'clock p. m." West's Ann.Pen. Code, §§ 1529, 1533.

Evelle J. Younger, Atty. Gen. of California, Edward P. O'Brien, Robert R. Granucci, Deputy Attys. Gen., San Francisco, for appellant. (11)

William F. DeLucchi, Regalado & Lindquist, Redwood City, for respondent.

Smith, Judge. (12)

The People appeal from a judgment dismissing an Information after suppression of evidence, where the evidence was obtained pursuant to a search warrant specifying "daytime" service, but which was served at 9:30 p. m. at night. (13) (14)

In 1970, section 1533 of the Penal Code was amended to eliminate the provision for "daytime" service for normal service of a search warrant. Instead of "daytime," the statute now specifies normal service as proper "between the hours of 7 o'clock a. m. and 10 o'clock p. m." Apparently by oversight, the Legislature neglected to also amend the mandatory provisions under section 1529 of the Penal Code, which continues to require "daytime" service. An inconsistency exists as to the mandatory requirements of search warrants unless section 1529 of the Penal Code is read as having been amended by implication when section 1533 of the Penal Code was expressly amended. Otherwise, the only warrant an issuing magistrate could authorize, without possibly violating one or the other statute, would be one for unlimited service at any hour of day or night upon a showing of good cause. Nothing suggests that this was the legislative intent. (15) (19)

The provisions of the Penal Code "are to be construed according to the fair import of their terms, with a view to effect its objects and to promote justice." (Pen.Code, § 4.) "In the construction of a statute the intention of the Legislature . . . is to be pursued, if possible; and when a general and particular provision are inconsistent, the latter is paramount to the former." (Code Civ.Proc., § 1859.) (16) (18) (16)

(10a) (1) Under the definition in Section 7 of the Penal Code, daytime is defined as "the period between sunrise and sunset." This general provision is clearly inconsistent with the particular provision relating to service of search warrants between the hours of 7 o'clock a. m. and 10 o'clock p. m. established under the amendment of section 1533 of the Penal Code. Under the general rules of statutory construction, we interpret "daytime" in the particular provisions of section 1529 of the Penal Code as having (18)

been impliedly amended to provide the same period for service as that under amended section 1533 of the Penal Code. (19)

". . . 'where the language of a statute is reasonably susceptible of two constructions, one of which in application will render it reasonable, fair and harmonious with its manifest purpose, and another which would be productive of absurd consequences, the former construction should be adopted.' (citation) ; and 'if certain provisions are repugnant, effect should be given to those which best comport with the end to be accomplished and render the statute effective, rather than nugatory.' " (Dept. of Motor Vehicles of California v. Indus. Acc. Com. (1939) 14 Cal.2d 189, 195, 93 P.2d 131, 134.) (18) (17)

(10a) (2) We hold that the People are correct in their assertion that service was valid since it was within the hours specified under amended section 1533 of the Penal Code. Any other holding would mean that section 1529 of the Penal Code would now require service at hours determined to be peculiarly abrasive and requiring a higher standard of proof (Tidwell v. Superior Court (1971) 17 Cal.App.3d 780, 786–787, 95 Cal.Rptr. 213) without a showing of good cause. (19) (18) (17)

This court has always been scrupulous in demanding a high standard for the admission of evidence pursuant to warrants. Our ruling today does not violate this standard. The integrity of our trial system in large measure depends upon the integrity of the evidence admitted at trial. The case before us deals with the timing of serving a warrant. If the case had involved other aspects of the warrant such as its specificity, our result would probably have been different. (21)

The judgment is reversed, and the trial court is directed to deny the motion to suppress the evidence. (20)

Jones, Judge (Concurring in result only). (22)

Thomas, Judge (Dissenting). (23)

If the California legislature intended to amend section 1529 of the Penal Code, it should have done so expressly. It is not the function of the judiciary to amend the statutes passed by the legislature. The public has a right to rely on the written language of statutes; in fact, we frequently admonish the citizenry if they ignore that language. For the courts to alter the language after the fact not only infringes upon the right of the legislature to be the sole entity under our system that can enact and amend legislation, but also is a signal to the public and to government officials that they can no longer trust the law as validly passed by the legislative branch. Both results are intolerable.

I would affirm the judgment below.

①   The California Reporter is an unofficial reporter of state opinions in California.   The "100" indicates the volume number of the reporter.[99]

②   The court opinion begins on page 600.   This is very important to note for citation purposes.   (Part of the unofficial citation of this case would be 100 Cal.Rptr. 600).

③   Normally when the "People" or the state brings an action, as plaintiff, it is a criminal case.   This is an appellate court decision.   Trial court decisions are appealed to the appellate court.   The "appellant" is the party bringing the appeal because of dissatisfaction with the ruling or decision of the lower court.   Hence California was the plaintiff in the lower court (Superior Court, County of San Mateo) and is now the appellant in the higher court (Court of Appeal, First District, Division 1.)

④   Bruni was the defendant in the lower court since he was being sued, or in this case, charged with a crime.   The appeal is taken against him by the People (appellant) because the lower court ruling was favorable to Bruni to the dissatisfaction of the People.   The party against whom a case is brought on appeal is called the "respondent."   Another word for respondent is "appellee."

⑤   "Cr. 10096" means the docket or calendar number of the case.   "Cr." stands for "criminal."

⑥   The first step that a researcher should take when reading a case is to make careful note of the name of the court writing the opinion.   As soon as possible, the researcher must learn the hierarchy of courts in his/her state as well as the federal hierarchy.   Normally, there are three levels of courts: trial level, middle appeal level and supreme level.   (Most cases are appealed from the trial court to the middle appeal level and then to the supreme level.).   Here, we know from the title of the court (Court of Appeal) that it is an appellate court.   It is not the supreme court because in California the highest court is called the California Supreme Court.

The name of the court is significant because of "legal authority."[100]   If the court were the highest or supreme court of the state then the case would be applicable throughout the state.   A middle appeals court decision, on the other hand, applies only in the area of the state over which it has jurisdiction.   (The jurisdiction of a trial court is even more narrow.)   When the reader sees that the opinion has been written by a trial or middle appeals court, s/he is immediately put on notice to check to determine whether the case was ever appealed subsequent to the date of the opinion before him.   This checking is called shepardizing.[101]

⑦   When a case is being cited, only the year (here, 1972) is used and not the month or day.   April 27, 1972 is the date of the decision.   Sometimes, the date of the hearing will be given as well as the date of the decision.   The latter date is still the critical one for citation purposes.

⑧   Here the editors provide the reader with a summary of what the opinion says.   The court did not write this summary; the editors did.   It is, therefore, not an official statement of the law.   It is merely an aid to the reader.   You may have many cases to read and time to read only a few.   You sometimes read this summary to let you know if the opinion covers the areas in which you are interested.

⑨   Here continues the unofficial summary, providing the reader with what procedurally must happen as a result of the April 27 opinion.

⑩ Here are more summaries. These are the editor's headnotes—again not the language of the court (the opinion has not yet begun). The editors first read the opinion and decide how many major topics are treated by the court. (The organization of the paragraphs is often referred to as the "syllabus.") Each topic is given a paragraph and a number. See ⑩ₐ in the opinion itself for the numbers [1] and [2]. These bracketed numbers correspond with the numbers of the headnotes.

The headnotes also have a topic and a key number, here "Searches and Seizures ⊂⇒3.8(1)." This paragraph will be printed in the digest system of the West Publishing Company. The headnotes serve two purposes. First, they are another summary of the points covered in the opinion and are a shorthand way of a researcher's finding out if it is worth the time to read or study the entire opinion. Second, the researcher can find out what other courts have said about the same or similar points in the paragraph headnotes by going to the digest system, looking up the topic and number of the headnote (here Searches and Seizures ⊂⇒3.8(1)) and reading summary paragraphs from other court opinions.[102]

⑪ Here are the attorneys that represented the appellant and respondent on appeal. Note that the attorney general's office represented the People. The attorney general or the district attorney's office represents the state in criminal cases.

⑫ The opinion begins with the name of the judge who wrote the opinion, Judge Smith. In this spot you will sometimes find the words "The Court," "Per curiam," or "Memorandum Opinion" meaning that the entire court (consisting of three to perhaps twenty-three judges) "wrote" the opinion. One judge wrote the opinion, but the court decided not to mention the name of any individual judge.

⑬ In reading or briefing a case, the first chore of the researcher is to make note of the judicial history of the case to date. The lower court dismissed the information (similar to an indictment) against Bruni after certain evidence was suppressed (i.e., declared inadmissible), and the People appealed this dismissal judgment.

If the words "Information" or "suppression" are new to you, look them up in a legal dictionary before proceeding. This is true of every strange word.

⑭ It is critical for the researcher to state the facts of the case. Here the facts are relatively simple: a search warrant that said "daytime" service was served at 9:30 p. m. and evidence was taken pursuant to this search warrant. Defendant objected to the admission of this evidence at trial. In most cases the facts are not this simple. The facts are sometimes given at the beginning of the opinion, as here, and other times they are scattered throughout the opinion. If you confront the latter situation, you must carefully read the entire case to piece the facts together. The facts are critical because you must assess how analogous the facts of your own problem are to those of the case you are reading (assuming that the issues in the problem are covered in the case at all). If your facts are the same or substantially the same as the key facts of the case, then the law of the case will probably apply to your problem. If the facts of your problem are somewhat the same and somewhat different from those of the case, then it is much more debatable whether the case is analogous and therefore whether the law of the case applies.

⑮   The next critical stage of reading a case is to state the issue (or issues) that the court was deciding in the case.   This is often a difficult task since many opinions are long and complicated.   Judges often ramble.   The researcher must be able to identify the primary issue that the court was deciding. The issue in People v. Bruni is not difficult to state: is evidence admissible which was obtained pursuant to a daytime warrant but served at 9:30 p. m. when there is an inconsistency in the statutes as to when service must take place?

The court does not quote extensively from any of the relevant statutes. You should find the full statutes in your library and read them on your own if you think it would aid you in following what the court is saying.   If for example, you want to read the entire version of section 1533 before and after the amendment, you would go to the California statutes, look up the Penal Code and find section 1533.   Depending upon how old the code volume is, you may have to check the pocket part to find the 1970 amendment.

According to the court, section 1533 is inconsistent with section 1529. Section 1529 requires "daytime" service.   The legal issue, stated another way, is whether 1529 was amended by implication.   If so, then the 9:30 p. m. search was valid (since service would be authorized up to 10:00 p. m.), and the evidence derived therefrom is admissible in court (if otherwise valid).

⑯   The court refers to other statutes to support the conclusion it will reach.   Note the interrelationship of the statutory sections.   One statute is interpreted by interpreting other statutes.   Section 4 of the Penal Code ("Pen.Code") says that the sections of the Penal Code are to be interpreted ("construed") rationally and according to common sense ("according to the fair import of their terms").   Section 1859 of the Code of Civil Procedure ("Code Civ.Proc.") says that when there is a general and a particular section that are inconsistent, the latter is preferred.

The sequence of statutory interrelationship in this case is as follows:

1. Section 1529 of Penal Code says "daytime;"
2. Section 7 of the Penal Code defines daytime as sunrise to sunset.
3. Section 1533 of the Penal Code as amended says 7 a. m. to 10:00 p. m.
4. Section 4 of Penal Code and Section 1859 of the Code of Civil Procedure provides principles of interpreting statutes that are inconsistent.

⑰   In the same manner, a court will refer to other cases to support its ruling.   In this way, the court argues that the other cases are precedent for the case before the court.   The court in People v. Bruni, therefore, is saying that Dept. of Motor Vehicles of California v. Indus. Acc. Com. and Tidwell v. Superior Court are precedent for its own ruling.

⑱   Here is the reasoning of the court to support its ruling.   If there is a general statute and a specific statute that are inconsistent, the court will adopt the interpretation that is consistent with common sense and the purpose of the statutory scheme.   Specific provisions are preferred over general ones.

⑲   The result or holding of the court's deliberation of the issue must then be weeded out of the opinion.   In this opinion, as in most, the result is stated in a number of places.   The result is that section 1529 was impliedly amended to authorize service up to 10:00 p. m.

⑳   The procedural consequences of the court's resolution of the issue are then stated, usually, as here, toward the very end of the opinion.   The judgment of the lower court is reversed.   The lower court cannot continue to suppress (i.e., declare inadmissible) the evidence seized at the 9:30 p. m. search.

An appeals court could take a number of positions with respect to a lower court's decision. It could modify it (e.g., reverse it only in part); it could remand the case (i.e., send it back to the lower court) with instructions on how to proceed or how to re-try the case, etc.

㉑ In theory, a judge must be very precise in defining the issue before him/her and in resolving only that issue. The judge should not say any more than must be said in order to decide the case. This theory, however, is sometimes not observed. Judges will get off into tangents, give long dissertations or "speeches" through their opinions. As indicated, this can make your job more difficult; you must wade through all the words to get to (1) the key facts, (2) the precise issues, (3) the precise reasoning and (4) the precise result.

The worst tangent that a judge can stray into is called *dictum*. Dictum is a judge's or court's view of what the law is or might be on facts that are *not* before the court. Judge Smith indicated that the result of the case might be different if the warrant was not specific; e.g., if it didn't name the individual to be searched or what the investigator was looking for. This was not the situation in the *Bruni* case, therefore his commentary or speculation is dictum.

㉒ On any court there may be several judges. They do not always agree on what should be done in a case. The majority controls. In *Bruni*, Judge Smith wrote the majority opinion. A concurring opinion is one which votes with the majority but which adds its own views about the case. In *Bruni*, Judge Jones concurred but specified that he accepted only the result of Judge Smith's opinion. Normally, Judges in such situations will write an opinion indicating their own point of view. Judge Jones did not choose to write an opinion. He simply let it be known that he did not necessarily agree with everything Judge Smith said; all he agreed with was the conclusion, i.e., that the warrant was validly served. It may be that to reach this result Judge Jones would have used different reasoning, relied on different cases as precedent, etc.

㉓ A dissenting opinion disagrees in part or in full with the result reached by the majority. Dissenting opinions are sometimes heated. Of course, the dissenter's opinion is not controlling. It is often valuable to read, however, in order to determine what the dissenter thinks that the majority decided.

Having studied the Bruni case in this way, the researcher should prepare a seven part brief:

1. FACTS: A search warrant that said "daytime" service was served at 9:30 p. m. Evidence was obtained during this search. The People (state) attempted to introduce this evidence at trial. Defendant Bruni objected.

2. JUDICIAL HISTORY: The trial court dismissed the Information against Bruni after refusing to consider the evidence seized pursuant to an improperly served warrant.

3. ISSUE: Is evidence admissible which was obtained pursuant to a daytime warrant but served at 9:30 p. m. when there is an inconsistency in the statutes as to when service must occur?

SUB-ISSUE: When Section 1533 of the Penal Code was amended to allow service between 7:00 a. m. and 10:00 p. m., did it impliedly also amend

Section 1529 which required daytime service?

4.   RESULT or HOLDING: Section 1529 was impliedly amended to conform to Section 1533.   The evidence seized pursuant to the search warrant can be admitted.

5. REASONING: Courts will try to reconcile statutes that are inconsistent. If a general statute is inconsistent with a specific statute, the court will adopt the latter whenever possible.

6. PROCEDURAL CONSEQUENCES: The trial court's dismissal of the information is reversed.   The trial must resume and the evidence cannot be excluded on the basis of the time of service.

7. SUBSEQUENT JUDICIAL HISTORY: As of the date of this brief, shepardizing shows no subsequent decisions in this litigation.

Note that the particular style or format in briefing a case is a matter of personal choice.   The important factor is to have all the components of a brief presented.   The order or format of the presentation is not significant.

FINDING CASE LAW

In searching for case law, you will probably be in one or more of the following situations:

- You already have one opinion on point[103] (or close to being on point) and you want to find additional opinions on point
- You are looking for opinions interpreting a statute, constitution, charter, ordinance, regulation or court rule that you already have
- You are looking for opinions containing common law (which is judge-made law in the absence of controlling statutory or constitutional law) and you have no such opinions to begin with

The following search techniques are not necessarily listed in the order in which they should be tried.   Your goal is to use all of these techniques.   In practice, you can vary the order of using the techniques.

First a reminder about doing the first level of legal research: background research.   You should review the checklist for background research presented earlier.[104]   While doing this research, you probably will have come across laws that will be of help to you on the specific facts of your problem (which is the second level of research).   If so, you may already have some case law.   You now want to find more.

TECHNIQUES FOR FINDING CASE LAW WHEN YOU ALREADY HAVE ONE CASE ON TARGET

1. *Shepardize the case that you have.*   (See Checklist #4a on shepardizing cases, supra p. 95.)   In the columns of Shepard's, look for cases that have mentioned your case.   Such cases will probably cover similar topics.
2. *Go to the West digests.*   There are two ways to do this:
   (a) Go to the table of cases in all the digests that cover the court that wrote the case you already have, e.g., the table of cases in the American Digest System.   The table of cases will tell you what key topics and numbers your case is digested under in the main volumes of the digest. Find your digested case under those key topics and numbers.   Look for other case law under the same key topics and numbers.

TECHNIQUES FOR FINDING CASE LAW—continued

TECHNIQUES FOR FINDING CASE LAW—continued

(b) Go to a West reporter (within the National Reporter System, supra p. 20) that contains the full text of the case you already have. At the beginning of this case in the reporter, find the headnotes and their key topics and numbers. Take these key topics and numbers into the digests of West to find more case law.
(See Checklist #2 on using digests, supra p. 81.)

3. *Find an annotation on your case.* Here you want to determine whether Lawyers Co-op wrote an annotation on your case within ALR, ALR2d, ALR3d, ALR4th or ALR Fed. Go to the table of cases found within the digests for ALR and for ALR2d. Also check the table of cases in the Quick Index volumes for the various sets, and a separate volume called ALR Fed. Tables of Cases, Laws, Regs (for recent federal cases). If an annotation has been written on your case, the case will be printed in full within one of the five sets of annotated reports, followed by the annotation with extensive cites to other cases on the same topic. (See Checklist #3 on finding and updating annotations, supra p. 86.)

4. *Find a discussion of your case in the legal periodicals.* Go to the table of cases in the Index to Legal Periodicals (ILP), the Current Law Index (CLI) and in the Legal Resource Index (LRI). There you will be told if your case was analyzed (noted) in the periodicals. If so, the discussion may give you additional case law on the same topic. (See Checklist #6 on finding legal periodical literature, supra p. 107.)

5. *Go to Words and Phrases.* Identify the major words or phrases which are dealt with in the case you have. Check the definition of those words or phrases in the multi-volume legal dictionary, Words and Phrases. By so doing you will be led to other cases defining the same words or phrases.

Now let us assume that you already have a statute and you now want case law interpreting that statute. The techniques for doing so are as follows (many of which are the same when seeking case law interpreting constitutions, regulations, etc.):

TECHNIQUES FOR FINDING CASE LAW INTERPRETING A STATUTE

1. *Shepardize the statute that you have.* (See Checklist #4b on shepardizing statutes, supra p. 99.) In the columns of Shephard's, look for cases that have mentioned your statute.

2. *Examine your statute in the statutory code.* At the end of your statute in the statutory code, there are paragraph summaries of cases that have interpreted your statute. Check these summaries in the bound volume of the code, in the pocket part of the volume and in any supplemental pamphlets at the end of the code. (See infra p. 122.) (For federal statutes, the codes to check are USCA and USCA supra p. 47.)

3. *Find an annotation on your statute.* If your statute is a federal statute, check the Table of Laws and Regulations Cited in ALR Fed found within a separate volume called ALR Fed. Tables of Cases, Laws, Regs. (See Checklist #3, supra p. 86.) If your statute is not a federal statute, you must check the various index systems for the five sets of annotations (supra p. 84) to see if there are annotations under the topic headings of your statute. Existing annotations will lead you to more case law on the statute.

4. *Find legal periodical literature on your statute.* There are three ways to do this:
   (a) Shepardize the statute. (See technique no. 1 above.) Citing material for a statute includes legal periodical literature.
   (b) Check the table of statutes in the Current Law Index (CLI), in the Legal Resource Index (LRI), and in the Index to Legal Periodicals (ILP). (Supra p. 105.)

TECHNIQUES FOR FINDING CASE LAW—continued

TECHNIQUES FOR FINDING CASE LAW—continued

> (c) Go to the subject indexes in ILP, CLI and LRI and check the topics of your statute.
> 5. *Go to loose leaf services on your statute.*   Find out if there is a loose leaf service on the subject matter of your statute.   Such services often give extensive cites to cases on the statute.   (See Checklist #5 on loose leaf services, supra p. 104.)
> 6. *Go to treatises on your statute.*   Most major statutes have treatises on them which contain extensive cites to cases on the statute.   (See Checklist #8 on treatises, supra p. 109.)
> 7. *Shepardize any cases you found through techniques 1–6 above.*   You may be led to additional case law on the statute.

Finally, we assume that you are starting from scratch.   You are looking for case law and you do not have a starting case or statute with which to begin. You may be looking for common law and/or for cases interpreting statutes which you have not found yet.

> ### TECHNIQUES FOR FINDING CASE LAW WHEN YOU DO NOT HAVE A CASE OR STATUTE TO BEGIN WITH
>
> 1. *Go to the West digests.*   CARTWHEEL your research problem (supra p. 70) to try to find key topics and numbers in the descriptive word indexes of the West digests.   (See Checklist #2 on using digests of West, supra p. 81.)
> 2. *Go to the annotations.*   CARTWHEEL your research problem to try to locate annotations through the various index systems of ALR, ALR2d, ALR3d, ALR4th and ALR Fed.   (See Checklist #3 on finding annotations, supra p. 86.)
> 3. *Treatises.*   CARTWHEEL your research problem to try to find treatises in the card catalog.   (See Checklist #8 on finding treatises, supra p. 109.)
> 4. *Loose leaf services.*   Find out if there are loose leaf services on the topics of your research.   (See Checklist #5 on finding loose leaf services, supra p. 104.)
> 5. *Legal periodical literature.*   CARTWHEEL your research problem to try to find legal periodical literature in ILP, CLI and LRI.   (See Checklist #6 on finding legal periodical literature, supra p. 107.)
> 6. *Legal encyclopedias.*   Go to the indexes of Am Jur 2d and CJS.   CART-WHEEL your research problem to try to find discussions in these legal encyclopedias through their indexes.   (See Checklist #7 on using legal encyclopedias, supra p. 108.)
> 7. *Computers.*   (Supra p. 112.)
> 8. *Phone and mail research.*   Find an expert.   (See Checklist #9 on doing phone and mail research, supra p. 110.)
> 9. *Words and Phrases.*   Identify all the major words or phrases from the facts of your research problem.   Look up these words or phrases in the multi-volume legal dictionary, Words and Phrases, which gives case law definitions.
> 10. *Shepardize.*   If techniques 1–10 above lead you to any case law, shepardize what you have found to look for more.   (See Checklist #4a on shepardizing a case, supra p. 95.)

Section P.   READING AND FINDING STATUTES

Here we cover four topics relating to statutes:

1. Reading statutes
2. Finding statutory law

3. Doing legislative history research
4. Monitoring proposed legislation

READING STATUTES

Below is an example of a statute from a statutory code.[105] The circled numbers are explained after the statute.

---

① ②

§ 146. Persons authorized to visit prisons

The following persons shall be authorized to visit at pleasure all state prisons: The governor and lieutenant-governor, commissioner of general services, secretary of state, comptroller and attorney-general, members of the commission of correction, members of the legislature, judges of the court of appeals, supreme court and county judges, district attorneys and every minister of the gospel having charge of a congregation in the town wherein any such prison is situated. No other person not otherwise authorized by law shall be permitted to enter a state prison except under such regulations as the commissioner of correction shall prescribe. The provisions of this section shall not apply to such portion of a prison in which prisoners under sentence of death are confined.

③

⑤

As amended L.1962, c. 37, § 3, eff. Feb. 20, 1962.

④

Historical Note **⑥**

L.1962, c. 37, § 3, eff. Feb. 20, 1962, substituted "commissioner of general services" for "superintendent of standards and purchase".

⑦

Derivation. Prior to the general amendment of this chapter by L.1929,

c. 243, the subject matter of this section was contained in former Prison Law, § 160; originally derived from R.S., pt. 4, c. 3, tit. 3, § 159, as amended L.1847, c. 460.

Cross References **⑧**

Promoting prison contraband, see Penal Law, §§ 205.20, 205.25.

Library References **⑨**

Prisons ⊂⇒13.
Reformatories ⊂⇒7.

C.J.S. Prisons §§ 18, 19.
C.J.S. Reformatories §§ 10, 11.

⑩

Notes of Decisions

1. Attorneys

Warden of maximum security prison was justified in requiring that interviews of prisoners by attorney be conducted in presence of guard in room, in view of fact that attorney, who sought to interview 34 inmates in a day and a half, had shown no retainer agreements and had not stated purpose of consultations. Kahn v. La Vallee, 1961, 12 A.D.2d 832, 209 N.Y.S.2d 591.

Supreme court did not have jurisdiction of petition by prisoner to compel prison warden to provide facilities in prison which would not interfere with alleged violation of rights of prisoner to confer in private with his attorney. Mummiani v. La Vallee, 1959, 21 Misc.2d 437, 199 N.Y.S.2d 263, affirmed 12 A.D.2d 832, 209 N.Y.S.2d 591.

Right of prisoners to confer with counsel after conviction is not absolute but is subject to such regulations as commissioner of correction may prescribe, and prisoners were not entitled to confer with their attorney privately within sight, but outside of hearing of a prison guard, when warden insisted on having a guard present in order to insure against any impropriety or infraction of prison rules and regulations during interview. Id.

①　Here you find the section number of the statute.　The mark "§" before "146" means section.

②　This is a heading summarization of what the statutory section is all about.　Section 146 covers who can visit state prisons in New York.　This summarization was written by the private publishing company and not by the New York State Legislature.

③　Here is the body of the statute written by the legislature.

④　At the end of a statutory section you will often find reference to the official edition of the section using abbreviations such as L. (laws), P.L. (Public Law), Stat. (Statutes at Large) etc.　Here you are told that in the Laws (L) of 1962, chapter (c) 37, section 3, this statute was changed or amended.　The Laws referred to are the Sessions Laws.　See the Historical Note ⑥ below for a further treatment of this amendment.

⑤　The amendment to section 146 was effective ("eff.") on February 20, 1962.　The amendment may have been passed by the legislature on an earlier date, but the date on which it became the law of New York was February 20, 1962.

⑥　The Historical Note provides the reader with some of the legislative history of section 146.　First of all, the reader is again told that section 146 was amended in 1962.　Note that in the second and third lines of the body of the statute, the title "commissioner of general services" is found.　The 1962 amendment simply changed the title from "superintendent of standards and purchase" to "commissioner of general services."

⑦　Also part of the Historical Note is the "Derivation" section.　This tells the reader that the topic of section 146 of the Corrections Law was once contained in section 160 of the Prison Law which dates back to 1847.　In 1929 there was another amendment.　The Historical Note was written by the private publisher and not by the New York State Legislature.

⑧　The "Cross References" refer the reader to other statutes that cover topics similar to section 146.

⑨　The "Library References" refer the reader to other texts that address the subject area of the statute.　On the left hand side, there are two listings, "Prisons" and "Reformatories" each followed by "key numbers."　The key numbers refer the reader to the digests of the West Publishing Company.　On the right column there is the abbreviation C.J.S. which stands for Corpus Juris Secundum, a legal encyclopedia.

⑩　The most important research reference is the "Notes of Decisions."　It includes a series of paragraphs that briefly summarize every court decision that has interpreted or applied section 146.　Of course, the decisions can only cover cases decided before the book was published.　For later decisions, the reader must look to the pocket part of the volume and to any supplemental pamphlets at the end of the code.　The first decision that treated section 146 was Kahn v. La Vallee.　Next is Mummiani v. La Vallee.　At the end of the final paragraph, you will find "Id" which means that the paragraph refers to the case cited in the preceding paragraph, the *Mummiani* case.

With this perspective of what an annotated statute looks like, we turn to some general guidelines to understanding statutes.

1. *Organizations of Statutes are Heavily Stratified.*

The codified statutes of a state can contain anywhere from five to one hundred fifty volumes.　The researcher, unfamiliar with a particular set of statutes, should look at the first few pages of the first volume. There s/he will usually find the subject matter arrangement of all the volumes that follow. For example, s/he may find "agency law," "correction law," "corporate law," "criminal law," etc. Different states have different labels and categorization schemes. Some jurisdictions may call each subject-matter a "code," e.g., "code of criminal procedure," "internal revenue code," etc. This is so, for example, with some of the statutes of Congress in the United States Code, and in the United States Code Annotated (USCA) and the United States Code Service (USCS).

The individual topics are further broken down into titles, parts, articles or chapters, which are then broken down into sections and subsections. Here is an example of a possible categorization for the state of "X:"

X code Annotated

Corporate Law
Title 1. (or Article 1 or Chapter 1) Forming a Corporation
Section 1. Choosing a Corporate Name
Subsection 1(a). Where to File the Name Application
Subsection 1(b). Displaying the Name Certificate
Subsection 1(c). Changing the Corporate Name

Note again however, that each jurisdiction may adopt its own labels. What is a chapter in one state may be called a title in another. Hence the first task of the researcher is to determine how the set of statutes s/he is studying uses its labels: law, code, title, article, chapter, section and subsection.

You also need to be sensitive to the internal context of a particular statutory section. A section is often a sub-sub-sub unit of larger units.

Example: section 1183 of title 8: Section 1183 is within Part II of Subchapter II which is within chapter 12 of title 8. (See illustration on page 125.)

As indicated earlier, a jurisidiction may completely revise its labeling system. What was once "Prison Law," for example, may now fall under the topic heading of "Corrections Law." This may not simply mean a change in labels; the numbering system may be changed as well. What was once section 73(b) of "Corporations Law" may now be section 13(b) of the "Business and Professions Law." If such a reordering has occurred, the researcher will be able to find out about it either in a transfer table at the beginning of the volume, or in the Historical Note at the bottom of the section.

2. *Topics in Statutes are Sometimes Arranged Chronologically.*
Statutes are mainly carried out by administrative agencies. The agency may be a grant making or service agency (e.g., social security administration, police department), or a regulatory agency (e.g., Federal Power Commission, State Utilities Commission). Statutes that cover agencies are sometimes organized chronologically in the sense that the statute will begin with the creation of the agency and move through to the point where a citizen terminates his/her relationship with the agency. The sequence may be as follows:
   a. the agency is created;
   b. the major words and phrases used in this cluster of statutes are defined;
   c. the agency is given a name;
   d. the administrators of the agency are given names and powers;
   e. the budgetary process of the agency is defined;

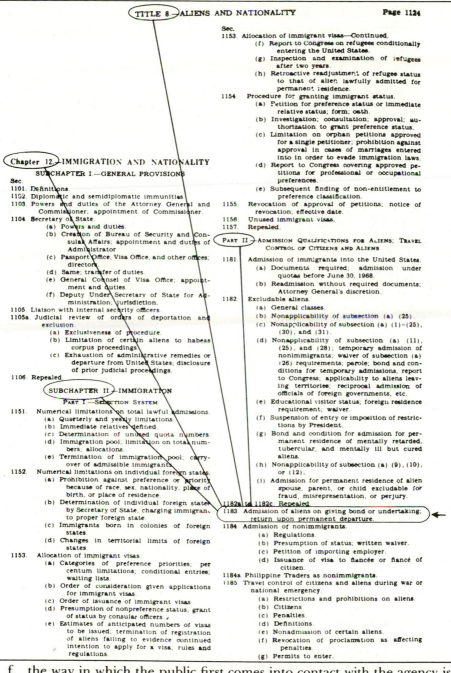

f. the way in which the public first comes into contact with the agency is defined, e.g., how to apply for the benefits or services of the agency;

g. the way in which the agency maintains its service is defined, e.g., how a citizen changes from one agency program to another;

h. the way in which the agency must act when a citizen complains about the agency's actions is defined;

i. the way in which the agency must go about terminating a citizen from its services is defined;

   j. the way in which a citizen can complain in court, if not satisfied with
       the way the agency handled his/her complaint, is defined.

This ordering of statutes, of course, is not always followed.   The chronological sequence is one example of how statutes are sometimes sequenced.

3. *All Statutes must be Based upon some Provision in the Constitution Giving the
Legislature the Power to Pass the Statute.*[106]

   Legislatures have no power to legislate without constitutional authorization.   The authorization may be the general constitutional provision vesting
all legislative powers in the legislature, or it may be a specific provision such
as the authority to raise revenue through issuing bonds.

4. *Statutory Language Tends to be Unclear.*

   Seldom, if ever, is it absolutely clear what a statute means or how it applies
to a set of given facts.   This is not always the result of poor draftsmanship
on the part of the legislators who are often asked to legislate for or against
unknown or undefined circumstances.   Because of this, they sometimes
"build in" ambiguity.   This factor, plus the ambiguity of words generally,
accounts for statutory language that regularly requires close scrutiny and
interpretation.

5. *A Central Concern in Reading Statutes is Determining What the Legislature
Intended.*

   It is appropriate for you to ask what is the common sense meaning of the
language in statutes.   You should then assess whether the legislature had the
same meaning in mind when it wrote the language.   Determining legislative
intent is one of the most difficult undertakings in the law.   When appropriate,
you may study the legislative history of the statute to determine its context.
Legislative hearings, for example, may have been held on the statute before
it became law.   Studying the transcript of the hearings and committee reports
on the subject, if any, and if available, will often shed light on what the
legislators were trying to do by passing the statute.   Such insights can be
helpful in understanding the meaning of the statutory language.   Then, of
course, there may be court opinions which provide judicial interpretations of
what the legislators intended by the statute.

6. *Statutes are to be Read Line by Line, Pronoun by Pronoun, Punctuation Mark
by Punctuation Mark.*

   Statutes cannot be speed read.   They should be read with the same care
that you would have to bring to bear if you were translating the language to
English from a foreign tongue.   All too often, for example, the careless
reader will read "or" when s/he should have read "and."

   Reading statutes is something that you must get used to.   The style of
statutory writing can be very painful.   Sentences sometimes appear endless
and there are often so many qualifications and exceptions built into the statute
that it appears incomprehensible.   The researcher who is confused and frus-
trated should not despair;   these are very natural and common feelings.   The
key is perseverance and a willingness to tackle the statute slowly, piece by
piece.

7. *Check to see if a Statutory Unit has a Definitions Section.*

   As indicated, codes are broken down into sub-headings called chapters, titles, articles, etc.   These sub-headings are sometimes further stratified into other units.   Very often at the beginning of each unit or topic there is a section of definitions.   This section will define a number of words that will be used in the remaining sections of the unit.   This section should always be read *before* the researcher studies any other section in the unit.   Here is an example of such a definitions section:

> **§ 31.   Definitions.**—As used in this article, unless the context shall require otherwise, the following terms shall have the meanings ascribed to them by this section:
>   1. "State" shall mean and include any state, territory or possession of the United States and the District of Columbia.
>   2. "Court" shall mean the family court of the state of New York; when the context requires, it shall mean and include a court of another state defined in and upon which appropriate jurisdiction has been conferred by a substantially similar reciprocal law.
>   3. "Child" includes a step child, foster child, child born out of wedlock or legally adopted child and means a child under twenty-one years of age, and a son or daughter twenty-one years of age or older who is unable to maintain himself or herself and is or is likely to become a public charge.
>   4. "Dependent" shall mean and include any person who is entitled to support pursuant to this article.

8.   *Statutes should be Briefed.*
     Briefing a statute simply means outlining it and breaking down its component parts in order to see it more clearly.   The following are some of the questions that the researcher could ask him/herself in briefing a statute:

   a. What is the citation (the name of the statutory code, volume of the code, number of the section, date of the code)?
   b. To whom is the statute addressed?   (to everybody, to the director of an agency, to citizens who want to do certain things?)
   c. Does the statute make reference to other statutes?   (if so, then the statute being read may be unintelligible without also studying the other statutes.)
   d. Is there a condition that will make the statute operative?   (very often the statute will have a "whenever" or a "wherever" clause indicating that whenever a certain set of facts occur, the statute will be applied; without the occurrence of the facts the statute may not apply.)
   e. What or who does the statute specifically *include* in its provisions?
   f. What or who does the statute specifically *exclude* from its provisions?
   g. Is the statute mandatory or discretionary?   (does it say or imply that someone "must" or "shall" do something, or does it say or imply that someone "may" or "can" do something?)
   h. Briefly summarize, in your own words, what the statute means to you.

FINDING STATUTORY LAW

TECHNIQUES FOR FINDING STATUTES
1. Go to the statutory code that covers the jurisdiction in which you are interested.   Some states have more than one statutory code.   For federal stat-

TECHNIQUES FOR FINDING STATUTES—continued

utes, there is the United States Code (USC), the United States Code Annotated (USCA) and the United States Code Service (USCS). (See supra p. 47.) You should use as many statutory codes as exist for a given jurisdiction. While they contain the same statutes, the index and research features will differ.

2. Read the explanation or preface pages at the beginning of the first volume of the statutory code. Also read the comparable pages at the beginning of the Shepard's volumes that will enable you to shepardize statutes in that code. These pages can be very helpful in explaining the structure of the code, particularly if there have been new editions, revisions or renumberings.

3. Most statutory codes have general indexes at the end of the set as well as individual indexes for separate volumes or for clusters of statutes within a volume. Use the CARTWHEEL to help you use these indexes, supra p. 70). Also check any tables of contents that exist. Some statutes have popular names, e.g., the Civil Rights Act of 1964. If you know the popular name of a statute you can find it in the statutory code in the code's popular name table. (You can also shepardize a statute by its popular name—see Shephard's Acts and Cases by Popular Name, supra p. 45.)

4. While reading one statute in the code, you may be given a cross reference to another statute within the same code. Check out these cross references.

5. Loose leaf services. Find out if there is a loose leaf service on the topics of your research. Such services will give extensive references to applicable statutes. (See Checklist #5 on finding and using loose leaf services, supra p. 104.)

6. Treatises. Find out if there are treatises on the topics of your research. Such treatises will give extensive references to applicable statutes. (See Checklist #8 on finding and using treatises, supra p. 108.)

7. Legal periodical literature. Consult the Index to Legal Periodicals (ILP), the Current Law Index (CLI) and the Legal Resource Index (LRI). Use the CARTWHEEL to these indexes to help you locate legal periodical literature on the topics of your research. This literature will give extensive references to applicable statutes. (See Checklist #6 on finding legal periodical literature, supra p. 107.)

8. Annotations. Use the various index systems for ALR, ALR2d, ALR3d, ALR4th and ALR Fed. The CARTWHEEL will help you locate annotations. Annotations will sometimes refer you to statutes—particularly in ALR Fed for federal statutes. (See Checklist #3 on finding and updating annotations, supra p. 86.)

9. Legal encyclopedias. Occasionally, legal encyclopedias will give you references to statutes. Use the CARTWHEEL for gaining access to Am Jur 2d and CJS. (See Checklist #7 for using legal encyclopedias, supra p. 108.

10. Computers. See supra p. 112.

11. Phone and mail research. Try to find an expert. (See Checklist #9 on doing phone and mail research, supra p. 110.)

12. For every federal statute that you find, determine whether there are federal regulations on that statute. To find out what federal regulations in the Code of Federal Regulations (CFR) are based on specific federal statutes in USC/USCA/USCS, check the Parallel Table of Statutory Authorities and Rules (Table 1) in the CFR Index volume.

13. Shepardize any statute that you locate through techniques 1–11 above. (See Checklist #4b on shepardizing a statute, supra p. 99.)

14. Check the legislative history of important statutes (infra p. 129).

15. Also update any statute that you find in the statutory code by checking the pocket part of the volume you are using, supplementary pamphlets at the end of the code, bound supplement volumes, etc.

16. Occasionally in your research you will come across a statute that is cited in its session law form. To find this statute in the statutory code, you must

TECHNIQUES FOR FINDING STATUTES—continued

> translate the session law cite into the codified cite. This is done by trying
> to find transfer tables in the statutory code. For federal statutes, a Statute
> at Large cite is transferred into a USC/USCA/USCS cite by:
> (a) Checking Table III in the Tables volume of USC/USCA/USCS (supra
> p. 100.)
> (b) Checking Table 2 in U.S. Code Congressional & Administrative News
> (supra p. 48.)
> Some session laws, however, never get into the statutory code. Hence there
> is no codified cite for such statutes. You must go directly to the session
> laws in the library—if the library has them. (For federal statutes, the session
> laws are in Statutes at Large.) It is also possible to shepardize session laws
> that are not codified.

DOING LEGISLATIVE HISTORY RESEARCH

For any statute that is important to your research problem, you must try to
uncover its legislative history. You want to know what happened before the
statute was passed. What process did it go through? What amendments
were considered and rejected? Were legislative hearings held on the proposed legislation? Were legislative committee reports written on the proposed legislation? Answers to such questions will often be helpful in understanding the intent of the legislature when it passed the statute.

In tracing legislative history, you are looking for leads to the documents
of this history, e.g., bills,[107] hearing transcripts, proposed amendments, committee reports. Once you find these documents, you read them to help you
interpret why the statute was passed and what its meaning is. These documents, for example, may tell you what the statute was *not* intended to do as
well as what it was trying to accomplish. Both kinds of information can be
very useful in interpreting the language of the statute that was eventually
passed.

Unfortunately, it is often very difficult to trace the legislative history of
state statutes. The documents are sometimes poorly preserved, if at all.
This is not so with federal statutes.

> ### TECHNIQUES FOR TRACING THE LEGISLATIVE HISTORY OF STATE STATUTES
>
> 1. Examine the historical data beneath the statute in the statutory code.
>   Amendments are usually listed there.
> 2. For an overview of codification information about your state, check the in-
>   troductory pages in the first volume of the statutory code, or, the begin-
>   ning of the volume where your statute is found, or, the beginning of the
>   Shepard's volume that will enable you to shepardize the statutes of that
>   state. (supra p. 96.)
> 3. Ask your librarian if there is a book (usually called a legislative service)
>   that covers your state legislature. If one exists, it will give the bill num-
>   bers of statutes, proposed amendments, names of committees that consid-
>   ered the statute, etc. If such a text does not exist for your state, ask the
>   librarian how someone finds the legislative history of a state statute in your
>   state.
> 4. Contact the committees of both houses of the state legislature that consid-
>   ered the bill. Your local state representative or state senator might be
>   able to help you identify what these committees were. If your statute is
>   not too old, staff members on these committees may be able to give you
>   leads to the legislative history of the statute. Ask if any committee reports
>   were written. Ask about amendments, etc.

TECHNIQUES FOR TRACING—continued

TECHNIQUES FOR TRACING—continued

---

5. Ask your librarian (or a local politician) if there is a law revision commission for your state.   If so, contact it for leads.
6. Is there a state law library in your area?   If so, contact it for leads.
7. Check the law library and drafting office of the state legislature for leads.
8. Cases interpreting the statute sometimes give the legislative history of the statute.   To find cases interpreting a statute, check the notes to decisions after the statute in the statutory code, shepardize the statute, etc. (supra p. 120.)   (See also Checklist #4b on shepardizing a statute, supra p. 99.)
9. You may also find leads to the legislative history of a statute in legal periodical literature on the statute (See Checklist #6, supra p. 107), in annotations on the statute (see Checklist #3, supra p. 86.), in treatises on the statute (see Checklist #8, supra p. 109), and in loose leaf services on the statute (see Checklist #5, supra p. 104).   Phone and mail research might also provide some leads (see Checklist #9, supra p. 110).

It is easier to trace the legislative history of a federal statute since the documents are more available.

TECHNIQUES FOR TRACING THE LEGISLATIVE HISTORY OF A FEDERAL STATUTE

1. Examine the historical data at the end of the statute in the United States Code (USC), and in the United States Code Annotated (USCA) and in the United States Code Service (USCS).
2. You will also find the PL number (Public Law number) of the statute at the end of the statute in USC/USCA/USCS.   This PL number will be important for tracing legislative history.   (Note that each amendment to a statute will have its own PL number.)
3. Step one in tracing the legislative history of a federal statute is to find out if the history has already been compiled by someone else.   Ask your librarian.   The Library of Congress compiles legislative histories.   If the statute deals with a particular federal agency, check with the library or law department of that agency in Wash. D.C. or in the regional offices to see if it has compiled the legislative history.   Also check with special interest groups or associations who are directly affected by the statute.   They may have compiled the legislative history which might be available to you. (One question you can ask through phone and mail research is whether the expert knows if anyone has compiled the legislative history of the statute whom you could contact.   See Checklist #9 on doing phone and mail research, supra p. 110.) Ask your librarian if there is a Union List of Legislative Histories for your area.   This List tells you what libraries have compiled legislative histories on federal statutes.
4. The following texts are useful in tracing the legislative history of federal statutes:
   * U.S. Code Congressional & Administrative News (see Table 4)
   * CCH Congressional Index
   * Congressional Information Service (CIS) Annual
   * Information Handling Service (legislative histories on microfiche)
   * Digest of Public General Bills and Resolutions
   * Congressional Record (see Index and the History of Bills and Resolutions for House and Senate)
   * House and Senate Journals
   * Congressional Quarterly
   * Congressional Monitor
5. Contact both committees of Congress that considered the legislation to ask for leads to legislative history.   (They may be able to send you committee reports, hearing transcripts, etc.)

TECHNIQUES FOR TRACING—continued

TECHNIQUES FOR TRACING—continued

6. Cases interpreting the statute sometimes give the legislative history of the statute.   To find cases interpreting the statute, check the notes to decisions after the statute in the USCA and in the USCS.   Also, shepardize the statute (see Checklist # 4b on shepardizing a statute, supra p. 99).   See also supra p. 41.

7. Find out if there is an annotation on the statute.   See the "Table of Laws and Regulations Cited in ALR Fed" in a volume called ALR Fed. Table of Cases, Laws, Regs.   See Checklist #3 on finding and updating annotations, supra p. 86.

8. You may also find leads to the legislative history of a statute in legal periodical literature (see Checklist #6, supra p. 107), in treatises on the statute (see Checklist #8, supra p. 109), in loose leaf services on the statute (see Checklist #5, supra p. 104) and through phone and mail research (see Checklist #9, supra p. 110).

9. Examine your statute in its session law form in Statutes at Large for possible leads.

MONITORING PROPOSED LEGISLATION

Occasionally you will be asked to monitor a bill currently before the legislature that has relevance to the law office where you work.   To monitor a bill means to find out its current status in the legislature and to keep track of all the forces that are trying to enact, defeat or modify the bill.

First, examine the process by which a bill becomes a law in the legislature. The legislature usually consists of two "houses"—often called the House and Senate:

1. A member of one of the houses gets an idea for a law;
2. THE idea is put in the form of a *bill*;
3. THE bill goes to a legislative committee of this house and this committee studies it and usually holds *hearings* on it;
4. THE committee makes its recommendation to the entire house; for example, the committee can recommend that the bill be approved or defeated;
5. THE entire house either accepts or rejects this recommendation and approves or defeats the bill;
6. IF the bill is defeated, that is the end of it for this session of the legislature;
7. IF the bill is passed by the house, it is sent to the *other* house;
8. THIS other house then sends the bill to its own legislative committee for study and hearings;
9. THIS committee makes its recommendation to the full house;
10. THE full house either accepts or rejects this recommendation and approves or defeats this bill;
11. IF this house defeats the bill, then that is the end of it for this session of the legislature—even though the other house approved it;
12. IF both houses have approved it, but still have differences of opinion in what the bill should say, the bill goes to a *Conference Committee* which is made up of members of *both* houses who iron out the differences of opinion;
13. THE Conference Committee then makes its recommendation and both houses approve or disapprove it;
14. IF either house disapproves the recommendation of the Conference Committee, the bill is dead for this session of the legislature;
15. IF both houses approve the recommendation, the bill is sent to the *Executive Branch* (to the President or Governor);

16. THE Executive leader signs it or *vetoes* it;
17. IF s/he signs it, the bill becomes *law*;
18. IF s/he vetoes it, the bill is dead—unless the legislature overrides (or defeats) the veto by repassing the bill through a ⅔ vote.

TECHNIQUES FOR MONITORING PROPOSED LEGISLATION

1. Begin with the Legislature. Find out what committee in each house of the Legislature (often called the Senate and House) is considering the proposed legislation. Also determine whether there are more than two committees considering the entire bill or portions of it.
2. Ask committee staff members to send you copies of the bill in its originally proposed form and in its amended form.
3. Determine whether the committees considering the proposed legislation have written any reports on it and, if so, whether copies are available.
4. Determine whether any hearings have been scheduled by the committees on the bill. If so, try to attend. For hearings already conducted, see if they have been transcribed (a word-for-word recording).
5. Find out the names of people in the legislature who are working on the bill: legislators "pushing" the bill, legislators opposed to it, staff members of the individual legislators working on the bill, staff members of the committees working on the bill.
6. The local bar association is probably interested in and has taken a position on the bill. Call the association. Find out what committee of the bar is involved with the subject matter of the bill. This committee may have written a report on the position of the bar on the bill. If so, you should try to obtain a copy.
7. Is there an administrative agency of the government involved with the bill? Do any of these agencies have jurisdiction over the subject matter of the bill? If so, find out who in the agency is working on the bill and whether any written reports of the agency are available.
8. Who else is lobbying for or against the bill? What organizations are interested in it? Find out if they have taken any written positions?
9. What precipitated consideration of the bill by the legislature? Was there a court opinion that prompted the legislative action? If so, you should know what the opinion said.
10. Are any other legislatures in the country contemplating similar legislation? Some of the ways of finding out include:
    (a) look for legal periodical literature on the subject matter of the bill (see Checklist #6, supra p. 107);
    (b) check loose-leaf services, if any, covering the subject matter of the bill (see Checklist #5, supra p. 104)—these services often cover proposed legislation in the various legislatures;
    (c) check treatises on the area (see Checklist #8, supra p. 109);
    (d) organizations such as bar associations, public interest groups, business associations, etc. often assign staff members to do this kind of state-by-state research on what the legislatures are doing—such organizations may be willing to share this research with you;
    (e) find out if there is a Council of State Governments in your area—it may have done the same research mentioned in (d) above.

Section Q.   READING AND FINDING CONSTITUTIONAL LAW

READING CONSTITUTIONAL LAW

Constitutional law (or charter law for some cities and counties) sets out the fundamental ground rules for the conduct of government in the geographical area covered by the constitution.   It defines the branches of the government, establishes basic rights of citizens and addresses problems that the framers concluded had to be handled constitutionally rather than through the statutory, judicial or administrative process.   In reading constitutional law, a number of guidelines can be helpful:

1.   *Determine What Geographical Area the Constitution Controls.*
  A citizen could fall under three separate constitutions:
  a. The charter of his/her city or town;
  b. The constitution of his state;
  c. The constitution of the United States.

2.   *Thumb Through the Headings of the Constitution or Glance Through the Table of Contents.*
  How is the document organized?   What subjects did the framers want covered by the constitution?   A quick scanning of the section headings or table of contents is a good way to get a feel for the structure of the text, and this should be done *before* the researcher zeros into the particular problem being researched.

3.   *The Critical Sections or Articles are Those That Establish and Define the Powers of the Legislative, Judicial and Executive Branches of Government in the Jurisdiction Covered by the Constitution.*
  Who passes, interprets and executes the law?   For the United States Constitution, "all legislative Powers granted herein shall be vested in a Congress" (Article one, section one);   "the judicial Power of the United States, shall be vested in one supreme Court, and in such inferior Courts as the Congress may from time to time ordain and establish" (Article three, section one);   and "the executive Power shall be vested in a President of the United States of America" (Article two, section one).   The exact scope of these powers, as enunciated elsewhere in the constitution, has been and continues to be an arena of constant controversy and litigation.

4.   *The Amendments to the Constitution Define or Change or Add to the Body of the Text.*
  The main vehicle for changing the constitution is the amendment process which itself is defined in the constitution.   Some constitutions, for example, can be amended by a vote of the people in a general election.   A condition for most amendments is that they must be approved by one or more sessions of the legislature.   Constitutional amendments usually appear at the end of the document.

5.   *Constitutions are Designed to be All-Inclusive.*
  Every act of government and every right of a citizen should in some way have a foundation in the constitution.   Considerable interpretation of the constitution is necessary in order for this to be so, given the truth of the guideline that follows.

6.   *Constitutional Law is Written in Very Broad Terms.*
  There are, of course, exceptions to this, particularly with respect to the constitutions of local governments.   In the main, however, a common characteristic of constitutional provisions is their broad language.   How would you interpret the following section?

United States Constitution

"Congress shall make no law respecting an establishment of religion, or prohibiting the free exercise thereof; or abridging the freedom of speech, or of the press; or of the right of the people to assemble, and to petition the Government for a redress of grievances."

How many words in this provision do you *not* understand?   What is an "establishment?"   If the School Board has students reciting the Lord's Prayer at the beginning of each day, is the School Board establishing a religion? What does "abridging" mean?   If a government official leaks official documents to the press and the government tries to sue the press to prevent the publication of the documents, has the "freedom" of the press been abridged? If the people have a right to "assemble," could the government pass a law prohibiting all gatherings of three or more people at any place within 1,000 yards of the White House gates?   The questions arising from the interpretation of constitutional law are endless; tens of thousands of written court opinions exist on questions such as these.

7. *Constitutional Provisions Require Constant Interpretation Because of Their Ambiguity.*

The broader the language, the more ambiguous it is, and therefore the greater is the need for interpretation.   This, of course, does not mean that anyone can interpret the constitution any way s/he wants to and get away with it.   As indicated, numerous court opinions exist interpreting constitutional provisions.   These opinions must be consulted before one can intelligently talk about the constitution.   The existence of so many judicial interpretations does not, however, eliminate the need for the researcher to identify ambiguity in the constitution.   Court opinions do *not* cover every problem that arises today, and furthermore, the opinions themselves are often ambiguous.

8. *There are Two Schools of Thought on Interpreting the Constitution: The Liberal Versus the Strict Constructionist or Conservative School.*
(Note: the liberal/conservative terminology used here does *not* necessarily refer to political philosophy.)

A strict constructionist or a conservative is often very literal in his/her interpretation of the constitution, whereas a liberal tends to give constitutional language a broad application.   The issue of birth control information is an example of how these two schools of thought might clash.   Suppose a state passes a law forbidding a doctor from giving information on artificial birth control to citizens of that state.   The constitution obviously says nothing about artificial birth control.   At the time the constitution was written, modern birth control devices were unknown.   Does a citizen have a constitutional *right* to receive such information?

A strict constructionist might argue that since the right is not expressly established in the constitution, the state can regulate the dissemination of that information, e.g., by forbidding its dissemination.

A liberal on the other hand, might interpret some broad language in the constitution (e.g., "due process of law") to include the right to receive the information.   S/he would argue that the framers of the constitution meant it to be a flexible document which could be adjusted to meet current problems.   To this argument, the strict constructionist might reply that if someone wants to have a constitutional right to receive the information, s/he should try to amend the constitution to put it in, and not try to force it in by broad interpretation of the language.

9. *A Central Question for the Interpreter of Constitutional Law is: What Meaning Did the Authors Intend?*

Common sense dictates that when language is ambiguous, the ambiguity may be resolved by attempting to determine what the author of the language intended by it.   What was the author's meaning?   In what context was the author writing?   Does the context shed any light on what was meant?   This kind of analysis is fundamental to legal reasoning whether the document is a constitution, a statute, a regulation, or a case.   It is particularly difficult to do, however, with most constitutions written over a hundred years ago.   The intention of the authors or framers of the phrase "establishment of religion," for example, is not easy to determine.

FINDING CONSTITUTIONAL LAW

TECHNIQUES FOR FINDING CONSTITUTIONAL LAW
1. Start with the text of the constitution itself.   It is usually found at the beginning of the statutory code of the jurisdiction.   (The federal constitution is in USC/USCA/USCS, supra p. 47.)
2. Use the CARTWHEEL to help you use the general index of the statutory code and the separate indexes for the constitution itself, supra p. 70.   Also check the table of contents material for the constitution in the statutory code.
3. Following the text of individual constitutional provisions there are often notes to decisions containing summaries of cases interpreting the constitution.   Some of these notes can run hundreds of pages.   Check the separate index material for these notes (again using the CARTWHEEL).
4. Shepardize the constitutional provision.   The set of Shepard's to use is the same set you use for shepardizing a statute (supra p. 96).
5. Annotations.   Find annotations on the constitutional provisions in which you are interested.   The CARTWHEEL will help you use the various index systems that exist for the annotations in ALR, ALR2d, ALR3d, ALR4th and ALR Fed.   (See Checklist #3 on finding and updating annotations, supra p. 86.)
6. Digests.   Go to the various digests of West that cover the jurisdiction of your constitution.   (The American Digest System, of course, covers all jurisdictions.)   The CARTWHEEL will help you use the Descriptive Word Index of a digest to locate key topics and numbers on point.   (See Checklist #2 on using West digests, supra p. 81.)   (For cases on the U.S. Constitution, you can also go to the non-West digest—the United States Supreme Court Digest, Lawyers Edition, published by Lawyers Co-op.)
7. Treatises.   Find treatises on the entire constitution or on the specific portions of the constitution in which you are interested.   (See Checklist #8 on finding treatises, supra p. 109.)
8. Legal periodical literature.   Go to the three indexes to legal periodical literature: ILP, CLI and LRI.   Use the CARTWHEEL to help you locate periodical literature on the constitution.   (See Checklist #6 on finding legal periodical literature, supra p. 107).
9. Loose leaf services.   Find out if there are loose leaf services on the area of the constitution in which you are interested.   (See Checklist #5 on loose leaf services, supra p. 104.)

TECHNIQUES FOR FINDING CONSTITUTIONAL LAW—continued

TECHNIQUES FOR FINDING CONSTITUTIONAL LAW—continued

> 10. Phone and mail research.   Contact an expert.   (See checklist #9 on phone and mail research, supra p. 110.)
> 11. Words and Phrases.   Identify specific words or phrases within the constitutional provision you are examining.   Find court definitions of these words or phrases in the multi-volume legal dictionary, Words and Phrases.
> 12. Legal Encyclopedias.   Use the CARTWHEEL to help you locate discussions of constitutional law in Am Jur 2d and in CJS.   (See Checklist #7 on legal encyclopedias, supra p. 108.)
> 13. Shepardize every case you found through the above techniques that interprets the constitution.   (See Checklist #4a on shepardizing a case, supra p. 95.)
> 14. Ask your librarian how you can trace the constitutional history of a provision of the constitution (i.e., the equivalent of the legislative history of a statute). Many of the above techniques will lead you to material that also discusses constitutional history, particularly cases interpreting the constitution and legal periodical literature on the constitution.   There may, however, be additional sources to check.   Ask the librarian.

Section R.   READING AND FINDING ADMINISTRATIVE LAW

READING ADMINISTRATIVE LAW

A regulation is an official rule of an administrative agency.   Just as the legislature passes statutes, so the agency passes regulations.   The regulations of agencies are referred to as quasi-legislation because of their similarity to the statutes of legislatures.

1. *Regulations are Sometimes Organized into Chapters, Sub-Chapters, Parts, Sections.*

See Section P above on the organization of statutes.[108]   The same guidelines apply to regulations.   Unfortunately, however, regulations are not as well organized as statutes usually are.   There are many agencies writing regulations.   Few of them have coherent systems of organizing and distributing the regulations.   A major exception is the federal agencies, many of whose regulations are first published in the Federal Register and then codified in the Code of Federal Regulations.

2. *Regulations should be Briefed.*

Use the same briefing model described for statutes in Section P above.[109]

3. *Agency Regulations are Based on Statutes.*

Normally an agency does not have the power to write regulations unless it has specific statutory authority to do so.   An examination of the statute giving the agency this authority can be helpful in understanding the regulations themselves.

More broadly, the function of the agency is to carry out the legislative mandates of the statutes; administrators must carry out the law as defined for them in the statutes.   Hence, the researcher should be familiar with the statutory foundation of the agency not only to place the regulations in context, but also to be constantly conscious of an overriding issue: Is the agency carrying out or violating the intent of the legislature as defined in the statutes?

4. *Regulations are Designed to Translate the Policy Guidelines of Statutes into the Details of Running an Agency.*

In theory, the legislature in its statutes sets out the purpose of the agency and defines its overall policies, but leaves to the agency, through its regulations, the task of filling in the specifics of administration.   Regulations, therefore, tend to be very detailed.

5. *Regulations are often Unclear.*

Detail does not necessarily mean clarity.   Ambiguity in regulations exists and it is the job of the researcher to deal with it.

6. *Regulations are often Organized Chronologically.*

Just as statutes defining the roles of an agency are sometimes arranged chronologically, regulations tend to follow the same pattern.   Regulations so organized will begin by describing the process of application for services and run through termination.[110]

7. *Regulations should be Read in Segments, Piece by Piece.*

See Section P on reading statutes segment by segment.[111]   The same guidelines apply to reading regulations.

The other major kind of administrative law is the administrative decision which is a written resolution of controversies brought before the administrative agency.   Not many agencies publish their decisions in any systematic order; some agencies do not publish them at all.   Regulatory agencies such as the Federal Communication Commission and a state environmental agency usually do better jobs at publishing their decisions than other agencies.   Administrative decisions should be briefed in the same way that court opinions are briefed.[112]

FINDING ADMINISTRATIVE LAW

TECHNIQUES FOR FINDING ADMINISTRATIVE LAW
1. Start with the agency itself.   Call or visit the agency.   Many may have regional offices near you.   Contact the library, or the law department, or the public information section.   Ask for a list of the publications of the agency, e.g., regulations, decisions, annual reports, etc.   Also ask where these materials are located.   Find out if you can come to the agency and read them. Also ask about brochures describing the agency's functions which can be sent to you.
2. Whenever an agency official is reluctant to let you have access to any publications of the agency, you may have to do separate research as to whether you are entitled to access, e.g., under the federal freedom of information act and its state equivalents.
3. Many federal administrative regulations are printed in the Code of Federal Regulations (CFR) which are usually first printed in their proposed form in the Federal Register before they are enacted by the agency.   The CFR comes out in a new edition every year, supra p. 13.   Check the index volume of the CFR (using the CARTWHEEL, supra p. 70) to help you locate regulations on point.   Also check the monthly, quarterly and annual index to the Federal Register.   If there are no federal regulations on point in the Code of Federal Regulations or in the Federal Register, you must check whether the agency has regulations or rules, bulletins, etc. that are published elsewhere.   See technique no. 1 above.

TECHNIQUES FOR FINDING ADMINISTRATIVE LAW—continued

TECHNIQUES FOR FINDING ADMINISTRATIVE LAW—continued

4. Once you have found a federal regulation on point in the CFR, do the following:
   (a) Shepardize the regulation. (See Checklist #4c on shepardizing a regulation, supra p. 102.)
   (b) Find the statutory authority for that regulation. There should be an "authority" reference beneath the specific regulation in CFR *or* at the beginning of the cluster of regulations of which your regulation is a part. The authority reference will be to a USC cite which is the basis of the regulation. Go to the USC/USCA/USCS and read this statute. Make sure the regulation does not contradict or otherwise violate the statute that the regulation is supposed to implement.
   (c) Find out if the regulation has been *affected* in any way (e.g., change, addition, renumbering) by subsequent material printed in the Federal Register. This is done by checking your CFR cite in:
      (i) the LSA pamphlet (List of Sections Affected) at the end of the CFR, and in,
      (ii) the lists of CFR Parts Affected (daily and monthly) in the daily Federal Register from the date of the LSA pamphlet to the current date.
      The LSA pamphlet and the CFR Parts Affected will tell you on what pages of the Federal Register there is material that affects the cite of your regulation in CFR. (You only have to do this in between the date of the CFR edition you are using and the date of the next yearly CFR edition since anything affecting the regulation during the preceding year will be incorporated in the next edition).
   (d) Find out if there is an annotation on your regulation by checking the Table of Laws and Regulations Cited in ALR Federal which is found in a volume called ALR Fed. Table of Cases, Laws, Regs, supra p. 510.
5. State administrative agency regulations are much more difficult to find and update. A few states have an administrative code similar to the CFR. For most state agencies, you must check with your law library and with the agency itself (see no. 1 above) on how the regulations are printed, found and updated.
6. Federal or state administrative decisions are usually printed, if at all, in separate volumes for that agency.

Section S.   FINDING LOCAL LAW

Difficulties sometimes exist finding local charters, ordinances, etc. There may be a municipal code for your city or county containing such laws. Many charters are also printed in the state's statutory code. Check with your law librarian. Also call city hall, the city council or the county commissioner office. Speak to the public information officer or the law department. Ask about the local publications of your city or county. What is printed? Where is it found? How often is it printed?

Other items to check:

- Legal periodical literature on local law (see Checklist #6 on legal periodical literature, supra p. 107)
- The Shepard's volumes for a particular state will enable you to shepardize local charters and ordinances
- Case law on charters and ordinances; use the digests (see Checklist #2 on digests, supra p. 81)
- Annotations on local law in ALR, ALR2d, ALR3d, ALR4th and ALR Fed (see Checklist #3 on annotations, supra p. 86.)

- Treatises on local law (see Checklist #8 on treatises, supra p. 109)
- Am Jur 2d and CJS discussions on local law (see Checklist #7 on legal encyclopedia, supra p. 108)
- Loose leaf services may cover aspects of local law (see Checklist #5 on loose leaf services, supra p. 104)
- Phone-and-mail research—contact an expert (see Checklist #9 on phone and mail research, supra p. 110)
- Ordinance Law Annotations (published by Shepard's)

Section T.   FINDING RULES OF COURT

You must always check the rules of court governing practice and procedure before a particular court, e.g., on how to file a request for an extension of time, on the number of days a defendant has to answer a complaint, on the format of a complaint, etc.

TECHNIQUES FOR FINDING RULES OF COURT

Rules of Court for State Courts:
- Check your state statutory code
- Check individual rules volumes or services
- Check the desk copy of court rules[113]
- Shepardize rules of court in the same set of Shepard's you use to shepardize a statute
- For more case law on the rules of court, check the digests for your state (see Checklist #2 on digests, supra p. 81)
- Check local practice books or formbooks[114]
- Check with an expert (see Checklist #9 on phone-and-mail research, supra p. 110).

Rules of Court for Federal Courts:
- Check the USC/USCA/USCS, e.g., title 28
- Check individual rules volumes or services
- Check the desk copy of court rules[115]
- Shepardize federal rules of court in United States Citations, Statute Edition[116]
- For more case law on rules of court, check the digests (e.g., Federal Practice Digest 2d)(see Checklist #2 on digests, supra p. 81)
- Check the Federal Rules Service
- Check special treatises on the federal rules such as
  Moore's Federal Practice
  Wright and Miller, Federal Practice and Procedure
- Check annotations on the federal rules, e.g., in the Table of Laws and Regulations Cited in ALR Fed found in ALR Fed. Table of Cases, Laws, Regs. (see Checklist #3, supra p. 86)
- Check legal periodical literature on the federal rules (see Checklist #6 on legal periodical literature, supra p. 107)
- Check Am Jur 2d and CJS on the federal rules (see Checklist #7 on legal encyclopedias, supra p. 108)
- Check with an expert (see Checklist #9 on phone-and-mail research, supra p. 110)

Section U. FINDING INTERNATIONAL LAW

TECHNIQUES FOR FINDING INTERNATIONAL LAW

1. In general:
   - the yearly U.S. Statutes at Large contain U.S. treaties (supra p. 436)
   - United States Treaties and other International Acts
   - Treaties and other International Act Series
   - Treaties and other International Agreements of the United States
   - CCH Tax Treaties
   - Treaties in Force
   - Department of State Bulletin ("Treaty Information")
   - United Nations Treaty Series
   - Catalog of U.N. Publications
   - DeLupis, Bibliography of International Law
   - Whiteman's Digest of International Law
   - Schwarzenberger's Manual of International Law

   For other texts summarizing and commenting on treaties and international law generally, see Checklist #8 on treatises, supra p. 109.

2. Legal periodical literature.   There is extensive literature in the periodicals on international law both in general legal periodicals and in specialty periodicals devoted to international law exclusively.   (See Checklist #6, supra p. 107.)

3. Loose leaf services such as CCH Tax Treaties mentioned above.   (See Checklist #5 on loose leaf services, supra p. 104.)

4. American case law on international law.   Check the digests.   (See Checklist #2 on digests, supra p. 81.)

5. Case law of foreign countries.   Statutory law of other countries.   Go to the international law section of a large law library.

6. Annotations on international law.   (See Checklist #3 on annotations, supra p. 86.)

7. Legal encyclopedias.   For material on international law in Am Jur 2d and in CJS, see Checklist #7, supra p. 108.

8. Phone-and-mail research.   (See Checklist #9 on contacting experts, supra p. 110)

9. See Restatement of the Law 2d, Foreign Relations Law of the United States.

10. Shepardize all treaties.   Go to Shepard's United States Citations, Statute Edition.

11. Martindale-Hubbell Law Directory—Digest volume.   Contains brief summaries of the law of most countries, supra p. 39.

Section V. THE THIRD LEVEL OF RESEARCH (VALIDATION): ENDING YOUR RESEARCH

Earlier, we mentioned the three levels of legal research:[117]

1. Background research
2. Specific fact research
3. Validation research

We already examined the steps to take in conducting background research on an area of law that is new to you.[118]   We also examined the techniques of specific fact research through the checklists[119] presented above in preceding sections 0 through U of this chapter.   If you have done a comprehensive job on the first two stages of research, you may also have completed most of the third stage—validation research.

At the validation stage, you make sure that everything that you want to use in your research is still good law. This means making sure that the law is current and has not been affected by any later laws that you have not found yet. A good way to approach validation research is to take the perspective of the other side. Suppose that you have written an appellate brief. It has been filed in court and served on the attorney for the other side. Your brief will be handed over to a researcher in the law office of your opponent. That person will do the following:

- read the full text of all primary authority[120] on which you rely in order to see if you have interpreted the statutes, cases, regulations, etc. properly, to see whether you have taken quotations out of context
- shepardize the statutes, cases, regulations, etc. that you cite in order to find out whether the law is still valid
- read the secondary authority[121] that you cite in order to see whether you have interpreted the treatise, law review article, etc. properly; to see whether you have taken quotations out of context
- look for other primary authority that you failed to mention
- look for other secondary authority that you failed to mention

Proper validation research means that you will be able to predict what this other imaginary researcher will find when s/he checks your research through the above steps. In short, at the validation stage of your research you must ask yourself:

- Have I found everything I should have found?
- Is everything I found good law?
- Have I interpreted what I found properly?

The answer to the first two questions should be no:

- if you did an incomplete job of CARTWHEELING the indexes and tables of contents of all the sets of books mentioned in the checklists and techniques in this Chapter
- if you failed to shepardize cases, statutes, constitutional provisions, rules of court, ordinances, treaties, etc. as called for in the above checklists and techniques
- if you failed to take other standard validation steps such as checking the List of Sections Affected material to update a regulation in the CFR[122]

When you start your research, the difficulty you face is often phrased as "where do I begin?" As you resolve this difficulty, another one emerges: "when do I stop?" Once the research starts flowing, you are sometimes faced with a mountain of material and still do not feel comfortable in saying to yourself that you have found everything there is to be found. The only guidance that can be given to you is: be comprehensive in following all of the checklists and techniques presented in this Chapter. With experience you will begin to acquire a sense of when it is time to stop. But it is rare for you to know this with any certainty. You will always have the suspicion that if you pushed on just a little longer you will find something new and more on point than what you have come up with to date. Also there is no way around the reality that comprehensive research requires a substantial amount of time.   It takes time to dig.   It takes more time to dig comprehensively.

Section W.   ANNOTATED BIBLIOGRAPHY

An annotated bibliography is a list of library material on a particular topic with a brief description of how the material relates to the topic.   An annotated bibliography on contributory negligence, for example, would list the major cases, statutes, periodical articles, etc. and explain in a sentence or two what they have to do with contributory negligence.   The annotated bibliography is, in effect, a progress report on your research.   It will give your supervisor the status of your research. (The following instructions mainly cover the preparation of an annotated bibliography for a topic that requires the application of state and local law.   The same instructions, however, would be used when doing the bibliography on a federal topic.   The exception would be instruction #9 which calls for local ordinances.   For all other instructions below, replace the word "state" with the word "federal" when researching a federal topic.)

INSTRUCTIONS FOR PREPARING AN ANNOTATED BIBLIOGRAPHY

1. CARTWHEEL the topic of your annotated bibliography, supra p. 495.
2. Annotated simply means that you provide some description of everything you list in the bibliography—not a long analysis, just a sentence or two explaining why you included it.
3. Hand in an outline which will cover what you find on the topic in the sets of books mentioned in the following instructions.
4. Statutes.   Go to your state code.   Make a list of the statutes on the topic.   If there are none, say so in your answer.   For each statute, give its citation and a brief quotation from it which will show that it deals with the topic.
5. Constitutions.   Go to your state constitution (usually found within your state code).   Make a list of the constitutional provisions on the topic.   If there are none, say so in the answer.   For each provision, give its citation and a brief quotation from it which will show that it deals with the topic.
6. Cases.   If you found statutes or constitutional provisions on the topic, check to see if there are any cases summarized after these statutes or provisions.   Select several cases that deal with the topic.   Go to the digests (supra p. 27, p. 32, and p. 79).   Try to find other cases that deal with the topic.   Select several.   If you find no cases, say so in the answer.   For each case you find, give its citation and a brief quote from the opinion which will show that it deals with the topic.
7. Key Topics and Numbers.   In instruction #6, you went to the digests.   Make a list of the key topics and numbers that you found most productive.   (See supra p. 27 and p. 79.)
8. Court rules.   Go to the court rules that cover courts in your state.   (Supra p. 41).   Make a list of the court rules, if any, that deal with the topic.   For each rule, give its citation and a brief quotation from it which will show that it deals with the topic.
9. Ordinances.   Go to the ordinances that cover your city or county.   Make a list of the ordinances, if any, that deal with the topic.   For each ordinance, give its citation and a brief quotation from it which will show that it deals with the topic.
10. Agency regulations.   Are there any agencies that have jurisdiction over any aspect of the topic at the federal, state or local level?   If so, list the agencies.   If your library has the regulations of the agencies, make a list of the regulations, if any, that deal with the topic.   For each regulation, give its citation and a brief quote from it which will show that it deals with the topic.

INSTRUCTIONS—continued

11. ALR, ALR2d, ALR3d, ALR4th, ALR Fed.   Go to these five sets of books. (Supra p. 83.)   Try to find one annotation in each set that deals with your topic.   Give the citation of the annotations in each set.   Flip through the pages of each annotation to try to find the citation of one case from your state court or from a federal court with jurisdiction over your state.   Give the citation of the case.

12. Law reviews.   Use the Index to Legal Periodicals (supra p. 105), or the Current Legal Index (supra p. 106) or the Legal Resource Index (supra p. 106) to locate three law review articles that deal with the topic.   Give the citation of the articles.   Put a checkmark next to the citation if your library has the law review in which the article is located.

13. Treatises.   Go to your card catalog (supra p. 78).   Find any two treatises (supra p. 48) that cover your topic.   Give the citation of the treatises.   Some-Sometimes you may not find entire books on the topic.   The topic may be one of the many subjects in the treatise.   If the card catalog does not give you this information, you may have to examine the treatise itself.

14. Loose-leaf texts.   Are there any loose-leaf services on this topic?   (Supra p. 103.)   Check the card catalog and ask the librarian.   For each loose leaf, give its citation and explain how it covers the topic.

15. Words and Phrases.   Go to this multi-volume legal dictionary (supra p. 36).   Locate definitions from court cases, if any, of the major words and phrases involved in your topic.   Limit yourself to definitions from court opinions of your state, if any.

16. Shepardize every case, statute or constitutional provision you find in order to make sure it is still valid and in order to locate other material on the topic. (On Shepard's, see supra p. 87).

17. Other material.   If you come across other material not covered in the above instructions, include it in the bibliography as well.

18. When in doubt about whether to include something in the bibliography, include it.

19. There is no prescribed format for the bibliography.   One possible outline format you can use is as follows:
    TOPIC: _____
    A. Statutes (Instructions 4 and 16)
    B. Constitutions (Instructions 5 and 16)
    C. Cases (Instructions 6 and 16)
    D. Key Topics and Numbers (Instruction 7)
    E. Court Rules (Instruction 8)
    F. Ordinances (Instruction 9)
    G. Agency Regulations (Instruction 10)
    H. ALR, ALR2d, ALR3d, ALR4th, ALR Fed (Instruction 11)
    I. Law reviews (Instruction 12)
    J. Treatises (Instruction 13)
    K. Loose-Leaf Texts (Instruction 14)
    L. Words and Phrases (Instruction 15)
    M. Other Material (Instruction 17)

ASSIGNMENT 6

Prepare an annotated bibliography on the following topics:
(a) Common law marriage
(b) Negligence liability of a driver of a car to his/her guest/passenger
(c) Sex discrimination
(d) The felony-murder rule
(e) Default judgment

(f) Negligence liability of paralegals
(g) Worker's compensation for injury on the way to work
(h) Fact situation assigned by your instructor

Section X.   RESEARCH ASSIGNMENTS

In your responses to the problems that follow, be sure to include citations that support every position that you take.   Also, on a separate sheet of paper list the research steps that you used in attempting to solve the problems raised, e.g., what is the name of the law books you consulted, what headings did you check in the index, etc.

In analyzing and researching certain problems, you may find it difficult to proceed unless you know more facts about the problem.   In such situations, clearly state the missing facts that you need to know.   You can assume that certain facts exist in order to allow you to proceed with the analysis and research so long as (a) you state what your factual assumptions are *and* (b) your assumptions are reasonable given the facts that you have.

7. In your state, what entity (e.g., legislature, committee, court, agency, etc.) has the authority to prescribe rules and regulations on who can and who cannot practice law?
8. List the kinds (or levels) of courts (local, state or federal) that sit in your state and identify the powers of each court, i.e., what kinds of cases does each court hear?
9. In your state, define the following words or phrases:
    a. summons
    b. in personam
    c. mandamus
    d. exhaustion of administrative remedies
    e. judgment
    f. jurisdiction
    g. warrant
10. Mary Adams works for a National Welfare Rights Organization chapter in your state.   She is not an attorney.   An N.W.R.O. member, Mrs. Peterson, has a complaint against a local welfare department branch concerning her welfare check.   Mary Adams goes to a Fair Hearing with Mrs. Peterson to represent her.   The hearing officer tells Mary that she cannot represent Mrs. Peterson since she (Mary) is not an attorney.   Is the hearing officer correct?
11. Using as many statutory codes of different states as are available in your law library (do not go beyond ten different codes, however), find out how old a male and female must be in order to marry without consent of parent or guardian in each of the states.   (Each state may or may not have the same age requirements.)
12. Go to any statutory code that has a pocket-part.   Starting with the first few pages of the pocket-part, identify any three different statutes that have totally repealed *or* partially modified the section in the body of the bound text.   Describe what the modification was.   (Note, that you may have to compare the new section in the pocket-part with the old section in the body of the text in order to be able to describe what the modification was.)

Using the law (i.e., constitution, statutes, cases, etc.) *of your state*, research the following problems:

13. John Jones was sent to a state mental hospital after being declared mentally ill. He has been institutionalized for five years (since 1967). In his own view he is not now mentally ill. The hospital disagrees. What can he do? What steps might he take to try to get out?

14. Peter Thomas is convicted of petty larceny. At the time for sentencing, his attorney asks the court to grant probation in lieu of a prison term. The judge replies, "Since Mr. Thomas has had three prior felony convictions (one of which for attempted rape), I could not grant him probation even if I wanted to. I sentence him to a year in prison." On appeal, the attorney argues that the judge was incorrect when he ruled that he had no power to grant probation to a person with three prior convictions. Is the attorney correct?

15. Mr. Peterson invites a neighbor to his house for dinner. Mr. Peterson's dog bites the neighbor. Is Mr. Peterson responsible for the injury?

16. Sam, age 15, goes to a used car lot. He signs a purchase agreement on a used car: $50.00 down and $25.00 a month for the next ten months. One day after the purchase, Sam allows a friend to drive the car. The friend demolishes the car in an accident. When Sam tells the used car dealer about the accident, he is told that he will still have to make all payments until the purchase price has been paid. Is the dealer right?

17. An elderly woman presented the following facts to you during a legal interview: that she and her husband moved into their house in 1946; that next to the house was a vacant lot; that she does not know who owns the lot; that she planted a small vegetable and flower garden on this lot; that she erected a small fence around the garden; that she has continued to cultivate this garden for the past 27 years; that neighbors regard this garden as hers; that since her husband's death last fall, men in the neighborhood have been trying to use the garden area for a place to store their old car parts; that she is troubled by this and believes that if she had any rights in the garden area, she could call the police if they bothered her again. What are her rights?

For the following problem (18) use federal law only—be sure to check regulations on point, if any.

18. Dorothy Rhodes and John Samualson are the parents of Susan Samualson. (Dorothy married Robert Rhodes after divorcing John Samualson). Dorothy died in 1967 after separating from her second husband. Susan's father has disappeared.

Mr. and Mrs. Ford were neighbors of the Rhodes. Susan lived with them for a long period of time while her mother was having marital difficulties. A court granted the Fords custody and guardianship in 1968. The Social Security Administration sent Susan the social security benefits she was entitled to on the death of her mother. In 1969, the Fords formally adopted Susan, but did not inform the social security office of this; they did not know that they had to. When the social security office learned of the adoption, they terminated the payments for Susan and informed the Fords that the money she had received since the adoption would have to be returned.

The Fords want to know what substantive and procedural rights they have.

19. Tom Smith owns a small shoe repair shop. The city sanitation department determines that Tom is a carrier of a typhoid germ. He himself does

not have typhoid fever but others could become infected with the fever by coming in contact with him.   The city orders Tom's shop to be closed.   He and his wife are not allowed to leave the shop until arrangements can be made to transfer them to a hospital.[123]

  a. Can the city quarantine Tom and his wife?
  b. If the Smiths enter a hospital quarantine, can they be forced to pay the hospital bill?
  c. Can the Smiths recover loss of profits due to the closing of their business?

20. The Henderson family owns a $40,000 home next door to a small grocery store.   The store catches fire.   In order for the firefighters to get at the fire from all angles, they decide that they must break through the Henderson home, which was not on fire.   Damage to the Henderson home from the activity of the firefighters comes to $4,000.   Who pays for this damage?

21. Bill and Mary are married with two children.   They are happily married except for one constant quarrel.   Bill is upset at Mary because she goes bowling every Friday night.   Mary is disturbed at Bill because he plays cards every Tuesday night.   To resolve their difficulty, they agree on the following agreement: Bill will give up his Tuesday night event if Mary will give up her Friday bowling.   On Friday, Mary stays home.   On the following Tuesday, however, Bill plays cards.   He declares that he wants to continue the card playing.   Mary on the other hand wants him to live up to his agreement. She brings a suit in court against him charging breach of contract.   What result?

22. After a series of serious accidents in which numerous riders are hurt, a bill is placed before the city council which would require all motorcyclists to wear protective helmets of specified dimensions at all times.   Is the bill constitutional?

23. As a measure to enforce a standard of dental care, a bill is proposed that all of the drinking water in the state be fluoridated and every citizen be required to visit a dentist at least once a year.   Is this bill constitutional?

24. Tom Jones has terminal lung cancer.   Modern technology however, can keep him alive indefinitely.   Tom requests that the hospital officials no longer use the technology.   He wants to die.   What are his rights?

25. Al Brown is seventeen years old.   He is a self-styled "hippie."   He refuses to take steady work.   His parents tell him that they will fully finance a college education for him.   He refuses.   The parents go to court and ask that their son be forced to go to college and avoid ruining his life.   What result?

26. In 1942 James Fitzpatrick died leaving an estate of $50,000.   The executor tried to locate the heirs.   In 1943 the Probate Court closed the estate and distributed the money to the heirs that were known at the time.   In 1973, an individual claiming to be an heir appears.   He wants to go to court to reopen the estate and claim his share of the inheritance.   What result?

27. The Board of Education is alarmed over increasing disturbances in the public schools.   A Board regulation currently exists which permits school principals to administer corporal punishment to unruly pupils.   The Superintendent of Schools proposes that the Board adopt a regulation which would authorize the school nurse, under the direction of the principal, to administer an oral tranquilizer to disruptive pupils to the end that they could be rendered

"relatively passive" and responsive to school guidance.   Discuss the legality of the regulation.

28. The state claims that welfare costs are bringing the finances of the state to the brink of bankruptcy.   It is proposed that all children of welfare parents be required to attend vocational classes as part of their regular school curriculum.   Discuss the legality of the regulation.

29. The United Kosher Butchers Association is accepted by most of the Kosher meat stores as the authoritative certifier that "all the religious requirements have been thoroughly observed."   The Associated Synogogues Inc. certifies caterers as authentic carriers of kosher food.   The Associated Synogogues refuses to certify caterers who buy meat from stores certified by the Butchers Association because the latter refuses to submit to supervision by the rabbinical committee of the Associated Synogogues.   Many caterers then withdraw their patronage from stores supervised by the Butchers Association. What legal action, if any, can be taken?

30. The town of Salem has a population of 2,000.   A group of avowed homosexuals move into the area.   They began to run for public offices with some success.   The oldtime townspeople become very upset.   A state law gives courts the power to hospitalize mentally ill individuals.   Part of the definition of "mentally ill" is as follows: "he evidences an inclination to sexual depravity such as child molestation, homosexuality and like perversions." The mayor of Salem files petitions in court to have the homosexuals declared mentally ill and institutionalized.   Discuss any law that might apply to these facts.

31. Mary Perry belongs to a religion that believes that medical problems can be resolved through spiritual meditation.   Her son Paul is ten years old. One day at school, Paul is rushed to a hospital after collapsing.   Mrs. Perry is called at home.   When she arrives at the hospital, she is told that Paul will require emergency surgery.   She refuses to give her consent.   The doctor tells her that if the operation is not performed within the next twenty-four hours, Paul will die.   Mrs. Perry responds by saying that "God will cure my son." What legal action, if any, can be taken against her?

REFERENCES

Beer, An Annotated Guide to the Legal Literature of Michigan (1973)

Boner, A Reference Guide to Texas Law and Legal History: Sources and Documentation (1976)

Cohen (ed), How to Find the Law (1976)

Davies, Research in Illinois Law (1954)

Fink, Research in California Law (1964)

French, Research in Florida Law (1965)

Gilmer, Legal Research, Writing and Advocacy (1978)

Henke, California Research Handbook, State and Federal (1971)

Henke, California Law Guide (1976)

Jacobstein and Mersky, Pollack's Fundamentals of Legal Research (1973)

Kavass, Guide to North Carolina Legal Research (1973)

Knudson, Wisconsin Legal Research Guide (1962)

Lebowitz, Legal Bibliography and Research: An Outlined Manual on the Use of Law Books in the Texas and Federal Courts (1957)

Mills and Schultz, South Carolina Legal Research Methods (1976)

Poldervaart, Manual for Effective New Mexico Legal Research (1955)

Price, Bitner and Bysiewicz, Effective Legal Research (1979)

Rombauer, Legal Problem Solving: Analysis, Research and Writing (1978)

Surrency, Research in Pennsylvania Law (1965)

Wallach, Louisiana Legal Research Manual (1972)

Werner, Manual for Prison Law Libraries (1976)

FOOTNOTES

1. Infra p. 112

2. Infra p. 106

3. Infra p. 106

4. Infra p. 112

5. Infra p. 152

6. Infra p. 111

7. Infra p. 118

8. Infra p. 57

9. Infra p. 130

10. Infra p. 69

11. Infra p. 79

12. Infra p. 104

13. Supra p. 5

14. Infra p. 140

15. Infra p. 87

16. Infra p. 92

17. Infra p. 96

18. Infra p. 113

19. Infra p. 116

20. Infra p. 118

21. Supra p. 40

22. Supra p. 41

23. Supra p. 16

24. Supra p. 37 and infra p. 104

25.   From Statsky, W. & Wernet, J., *Case Analysis and Fundamentals of Legal Writing,* pp. 26ff., 549ff.   (1977).

26.   Infra p. 92

27.   Supra p. 18

28.   Supra p. 5

29.   Supra p. 41 and infra p. 92

30.   Supra p. 17

31.   Supra p. 18

32.   Supra p. 27

33.   Supra p. 26

34.   Supra p. 48 and infra p. 129

35.   Supra p. 34 and infra p. 79

36.   Supra p. 27

37.   From Statsky, W., *Domestic Relations: Law and Skills,* pp. 7ff.   (1978).

38.   Supra pp. 36, 48, 37, 36

39.   Supra p. 50

40.   Supra p. 36

41.   Supra p. 15 and infra p. 108

42.   Supra p. 26 and infra p. 108

43.   Supra p. 70

44.   Supra p. 48

45.   Supra p. 14 and infra p. 83

46.   Supra p. 37 and infra p. 104

47.   Infra p. 105

48.   Infra p. 106

49.   Infra p. 106

50.   Infra p. 129

51.   Supra p. 48 and infra p. 130

52.   Supra 39

53.   Supra p. 50

54.   Supra p. 87

55.   Supra p. 27

56.   Supra p. 18

57.   Infra p. 15

58.   Supra pp. 32, 33

59.   Supra p. 31

60.   Supra p. 15

61.   Supra p. 6

62. Supra p. 51

63. Supra p. 15

64. Supra p. 18

65. Supra p. 47

66. Supra p. 13

67. Supra p. 17

68. Supra p. 64

69. Supra p. 27, and p. 79

70. Supra p. 14, p. 15, and infra p. 83

71. Infra p. 112

72. Supra p. 14

73. Supra p. 18

74. Supra p. 44

75. Infra p. 140, and supra p. 75

76. Supra p. 34

77. Supra p. 13

78. Supra p. 50

79. Supra p. 46

80. Occasionally, however, you will be shepardizing through the session law cite if the particular session law will never be codified.   Not all session laws go into the statutory code.

81. Supra p. 92

82. Supra p. 68

83. Supra p. 47

84. Supra p. 43

85. Supra p. 44

86. Supra p. 13, and infra p. 137

87. Infra p. 138

88. Supra p. 38

89. Supra p. 5

90. Supra p. 37

91. Supra p. 8

92. Supra p. 48

93. Supra p. 36

94. Supra p. 48

95. Supra p. 36

96. Supra p. 37

97. Supra p. 15

98. Supra p. 38

99. Supra p. 18

100. Supra p. 50

101. Supra p. 41

102. Supra p. 34

103. Supra p. 51

104. Supra p. 75

105. Supra p. 46

106. Supra p. 53

107. Supra p. 16

108. Supra p. 124

109. Supra p. 127

110. Supra p. 124

111. Supra p. 126

112. Supra p. 118

113. Supra p. 41

114. Supra p. 34

115. Supra p. 41

116. Supra p. 43

117. Supra p. 74

118. Supra p. 75

119. Supra p. 77

120. Supra pp. 50ff.

121. Supra p. 50

122. Supra p. 138

123. See Cooper, G., & Rosenberg, M., Institute for Legal Service Assistant Manual (1969).

Legal Writing ═══════════════ 2

There are a number of different kinds of writing within a law office:

1. Letters
2. Instruments
3. Pleadings
4. Briefs
5. Memoranda

1. *Letters*

Many "garden variety" letters are written in a law office every day, e.g., a letter requesting information, a letter requesting payment, a letter notifying someone of the fact that the office represents a particular person or company. A more involved letter is the "opinion letter" in which the office writes to its client explaining the application of the law and advising the client what to do. Such letters try to present technical material in a comprehensible manner. Unlike a brief or memorandum, the opinion letter will not make extensive reference to court opinions or statutes. The need of the client is for clear, concise, practical advice.

2. *Instruments*

An instrument is a formal document that gives expression to a legal act or agreement. Examples of instruments are contracts, deeds, wills, leases, bonds, notes, mortgage agreements, etc. Many formbooks[1] exist which provide models of such instruments. Rarely will anyone write an instrument from scratch. The starting point is almost always a standard form or model which is adapted to the particular facts of the client.

3. *Pleadings*

Pleadings are formal statements of claims and defenses which are exchanged between parties involved in litigation. The major pleadings are the complaint, answer, counterclaim, reply to counterclaim, cross claim and third party complaint.   Formbooks are also often used as the starting point in drafting pleadings.   Some high-volume litigation firms use computers or word-processing equipment to help prepare frequently-used pleadings.

4.   *Briefs*

The word brief has several meanings.

First, to *brief* a case is to summarize its major components (e.g., key facts, issues, reasoning, disposition).[2]   Such a brief is your own notes on a particular court opinion for later use.

Second, a *trial brief* is a set of notes that an attorney will write to him/ herself or how s/he proposes to conduct the trial.   The notes will be on the opening statement, witnesses, exhibits, direct and cross examination, closing argument, etc.   This trial brief is sometimes called a trial manual or trial book.   It is not submitted to the court nor to the other side.   A *trial memorandum* on points of law might be submitted, but not the trial brief which contains counsel's strategy.   (This trial memorandum, however, is sometimes referred to as a trial brief.   In such instances, the trial brief consists of arguments of law rather than the tactical blueprint for the conduct of the trial.)

Third, the *appellate brief*[3] is the formal written argument to a court of appeals on why a lower court's decision should be affirmed, modified or reversed.   It is submitted to the appellate court and to the other side.   The appellate brief is the most sophisticated kind of legal writing done in a law office.

The first appellate brief that is usually submitted is the appellant's brief. The appellant is the party initiating the appeal.   Then the appellee's brief is filed in response.   The appeal is taken against the appellee (sometimes called the respondent).   Finally, the appellant is often allowed to submit a reply brief to counter the positions taken in the appellee's brief.

Occasionally a court will permit a non-party to the litigation to submit an appellate brief.   This is referred to as an *amicus curiae* (friend of the court) brief.   This is permitted only when the appellate court is convinced that the non-party will be affected by whatever decision is reached.   The *amicus* brief advises the court on how to resolve the controversies before it.

Not all appellate briefs have the same structure.   Court rules often specify what structure or format the brief should take, the print size, number of copies to be submitted, etc.[4]   The following are the major components of many appellate briefs:

a.   Caption

The caption states the names of the parties, the name of the court, the court file or docket number and the kind of appellate brief it is. The caption goes on the front cover of the brief.

b.   The Statement of Jurisdiction

Here the prior proceedings in the litigation are summarized, pointing out how the case came before the appellate court.   The authority or jurisdiction of the appellate court to hear the case is presented.

c.   Table of Contents

The table of contents gives the page numbers in the brief where all the different portions of the brief are found.   Entries in the table include summary statements of the major arguments and the page numbers on which these arguments begin.

d. Table of Authorities

This table lists all the cases, statutes, regulations, administrative decisions, constitutional provisions, charter provisions, ordinances, court rules, and secondary authority[5] relied on in the brief. All the cases are listed in alphabetical order, all the statutes are listed in alphabetical and numerical order, etc. The pages numbers on which each of these authorities are discussed in the brief are presented so that the table acts as an index to these authorities.

e. Questions Presented

Here the issues before the appellate court are provided.

f. Statement of the Case

The major facts involved in the appeal are presented. (Some briefs also include here some of the information listed under the statement of jurisdiction above.)

g. Summary of Argument

The major points to be made in the brief are summarized.

h. Argument

Here the attorney explains the legal positions being taken. All of the primary and secondary authority relied upon is analyzed.

i. Conclusion

The conclusion states what action the attorney is asking the appellate court to take.

j. Appendices

The appendices contain excerpts from statutes or other primary authority, excerpts from the trial, charts or descriptions of exhibits entered into evidence at the trial, etc.

5. *Memorandum of Law*[6]

A memorandum of law is an analysis of legal authority governing one or more legal issues. It is generally the product of a fairly extensive research effort.

There are two kinds of legal memoranda:

a. the *internal* or *inter-office* memorandum; and

b. the *external* or *adversary* memorandum.

The primary feature of an *internal* memorandum is its objectivity. The purpose of the memorandum is to provide a *highly accurate* prediction of what the probable outcome of any future administrative hearing or court proceeding will be. The audience of your internal memorandum will be your supervisor or anyone else within your law office who is working on the client's case.

An *external* memorandum, by contrast, is not an objective document at all. Rather it is an adversary document which attempts to persuade the reader to adopt a decision favorable to the client. While the internal memorandum is intended to provide objective information, the external memorandum is calculated to provide effective persuasion. The audience of your external memorandum may be a hearing officer in an administrative agency (if so, it will often be called a hearing memorandum or a "points and authorities memorandum"), or a trial court judge (if so, it will often be called a trial memorandum). A trial memorandum is like an appellate brief in that both are advocacy documents directed to a court. An appellate brief, however, is more stylized in format and, of course, is not written for a trial court.

The distinguishing features of an internal and an external memorandum are outlined in the following chart:

CHARACTERISTICS OF INTERNAL V. EXTERNAL MEMORANDA OF LAW	
INTERNAL MEMORANDUM OF LAW	EXTERNAL MEMORANDUM OF LAW
1. Emphasizes both the strengths and the weaknesses of the client's position on each issue. (Objective) 2. Emphasizes both the strengths and the weaknesses of the opposing party's probable position on each issue. 3. Predicts the court or agency's probable decision on each issue. 4. Recommends the most favorable strategy for the client to follow.	1. Emphasizes the strengths but minimizes the weaknesses of the client's position on each issue. 2. Emphasizes the weaknesses but minimizes the strengths of the opposing party's position on each issue. 3. Argues for a favorable decision on each issue.

There are five *essential* components to every memorandum of law.   They are:

1. *heading*;
2. statement of the *issue(s)* being treated;
3. statement of the *facts*;
4. presentation and *analysis* of authority;
5. *conclusion(s)*.

Depending upon such factors as the length and complexity of the memorandum, the number of issues being treated, and the structural requirements of the intended reader, a number of additional components may be included. These are:

6. table of contents;
7. table of authorities cited;
8. summary of issues and conclusions;
9. counteranalysis;
10. recommended next steps.

These ten components, and the factors affecting their use, are discussed below.   If all ten components are used in a memorandum, they will *not* be presented in the above order.

1. *Heading.*
   The actual format of the heading of your memorandum will depend on the type of legal memorandum you are writing.   In an internal or office memorandum, you will normally use a relatively informal heading which will state:
   a. the name of the intended reader;
   b. your own name;
   c. the subject of the memorandum;   and

  d. the date on which the memorandum was completed and submitted.
  e. the office file number for the case.
The following sample heading illustrates how this information might be set forth in a heading for a memorandum written on behalf of client Brown who is suing Miller:

Office Memorandum

TO: MS. PATTERSON
FR: MR. JACKSON
RE: Availability of contributory negligence defense in Brown v. Miller.
DA: April 30, 1976   CASE NO: 76–42

    Note that the subject matter description in this sample does not merely identify the name of the client or of the client's case, but also briefly indicates the nature of the question which will be treated in the memorandum. This information is needed for at least two reasons. First, the average law office case file will contain a large number of documents, often including several legal memoranda. A heading which at least briefly indicates the nature of the subject of each memorandum makes it much easier to locate the memorandum in the client's file if necessary. Secondly, it is unlikely that the usefulness of your memorandum will end when the client's case is closed out. Many law offices maintain fairly extensive libraries of old office memoranda which are catalogued and filed by subject matter for reference in future cases. This avoids unnecessary and costly duplication of research time in the event that a similar question arises in a future client's case. The subject-matter heading on your memorandum facilitates the cataloguing and filing of your memorandum in such a library.
    The inclusion of the date on which the memorandum was completed and submitted is important for similar reasons. While your analysis and conclusions may have been very accurate at the time the memorandum was written, subsequent changes in the law may have occurred by the time the memorandum is next referred to. When the reader sees the date of the memorandum, s/he will know from what date subsequent legal research will be needed.
    In an external memorandum, a more formal heading is required. Generally the heading should include:
  a. the name of the court or agency to which it will be sent;
  b. the name of the case;
  c. the docket number;
  d. the title of the memorandum;
  e. an indication of which party is submitting the memorandum.
    If the memorandum is to be filed with a court (e.g., a trial memorandum), you should consult the rules of that court to determine whether they contain instructions on the format which the court requires such memoranda to follow. If the rules do not cover trial memoranda, it is usually safe to follow the same heading format that the court requires for pleadings and motions. The following format is typical of many courts:

SUPERIOR COURT OF THE DISTRICT OF COLUMBIA

CIVIL DIVISION

*

ROBERT G. BARNES
    Plaintiff   *

     v.   *   C–34553–75

GEMINI REPAIR SHOP, INC.   *
    Defendant

                      *

MEMORANDUM OF DEFENDANT GEMINI REPAIR SHOP, INC.

---

2.   *Statement of the Issue(s).*

    Every memorandum should clearly set forth the issue or issues being treated. In a relatively simple memorandum involving only one issue, it is generally a good practice to state the issue *first*, in order to give the reader a context in which to place the facts and analysis which will follow. In a more complex memorandum involving several issues, this is not entirely practical. If you state all of the issues at the beginning of the memorandum without repeating them in the body of the memorandum, it may make your analysis of the issues hard to follow. The reader will be forced, at the beginning of each portion of your analysis, to flip back to the beginning of the memorandum to review the particular issue being treated. For this reason, when writing a memorandum involving two or more issues, you should state each issue immediately before your analysis of that issue, rather than at the beginning of the memorandum. In place of the initial statement of the issue you should substitute a *summary of issues and conclusions.* (See infra p. 160.)

    One additional variation is commonly employed in stating the issue in an external or adversary memorandum. Although in the summary of issues and conclusions at the beginning of the memorandum the issue will be phrased as a question, the restatement of each issue immediately preceding the argument or analysis should be phrased as a *statement*. This is accomplished by rephrasing your statement of the issue in the form of the conclusion which you hope to persuade the judge or hearing examiner to adopt. The reason for doing so is the nature of the external memorandum: advocacy and persuasion. Instead of simply restating the question, you are telling the judge or hearing examiner *early* in the memorandum exactly what conclusion you believe s/he should reach.

    In an office memorandum or in an external memorandum, you will often have to state and discuss certain issues *on the assumption* that the court or agency decides against you on prior issues that you have stated and discussed early in the memorandum. Suppose that the client is a defendant in a negligence action. The first issue may concern the liability of the defendant: was the defendant negligent or not? In the first issue, the defendant will be covering the liability question and will attempt to demonstrate in the discussion or analysis on this issue why s/he is *not* liable.   All of the evidence and authority supporting non-liability will be treated in the most effective manner under this issue.   At the time that the memorandum is written, there will, of course, be no resolution of the first issue.   Hence, you must be prepared for issues which will arise *on the assumption* that you lose on the first issue.   For example, all issues concerning damages (how much money must be paid to a plaintiff who has successfully established liability) need to be anticipated and analyzed in the event that the liability issue is lost.   The statement of the damage issues in the memorandum should be prefaced by language such as:

> In the event that we lose the first issue, then we must discuss the issue of .   . ..

or

> On the assumption that the court finds for [the other party] on the liability issue, the question then becomes whether .   . ..

No matter how firmly you believe in your prediction of what a court or agency will do on an issue, be prepared for what will happen in the event that your prediction eventually proves to be erroneous.   This must be done in an internal memorandum, in an external memorandum (hearing or trial) *and* in an appellate brief.

3.   *Statement of the Facts.*

Your statement of the facts of the client's case is probably the most important component of your memorandum.   You should take great pains to see that it is concise, highly accurate, and well-organized.

   a. Conciseness.   An unduly long fact statement will serve only to frustrate the reader.   Try to eliminate any unnecessary facts from the statement. One way of doing this is to carefully review your fact statement *after* you have completed your analysis of the issues.   If there are facts in your statement which are not subsequently referred to in your analysis, it is likely that those facts are not particularly relevant to your memorandum and can be eliminated in your final draft of the memorandum.

   b. Accuracy.   In writing an appellate brief, you will find that your statement of the facts will be limited by the record and the findings of the lower court.   You will rarely be confronted with this limitation in drafting a legal memorandum.   In most instances you will be drafting the memorandum in preparation for going before the court or agency for the first time;   there may be no prior proceedings.   Hence there will be no record, and no official findings of fact.   The temptation will be to indulge in wishful thinking—to ignore adverse facts and to assume that disputed facts will be resolved in favor of the client.   Do not give in to this temptation.   You must assess the legal consequences of favorable *and* unfavorable facts.   If a particular fact is presently unknown, put aside your writing, if possible, and investigate to determine what evidence exists to prove the fact one way or the other.   If it is not practical to conduct an investigation at the present time, then you should provide an analysis of what law will apply based upon your most reasonable estimate of what an investigation may uncover.   The need for accuracy does not mean that you should not attempt to state the facts in the light most favorable to the client. It simply means that you must be cautious in doing so to avoid making false or misleading statements of fact.

c. *Organization.* A disorganized statement of facts will not only prevent the reader from understanding the events in question, but will also interfere with his/her understanding of your subsequent analysis. In general, it is best to start with a short one or two sentence summary of the nature of the case followed by a *chronologically* ordered statement of the detailed facts. Occasional variations from strict chronological order can be effective so long as they do not interfere with the flow of the story.

4. *Presentation and Analysis of Authority.*

It is generally best to begin this portion of your memorandum by describing and discussing the controlling law on the issue you are treating. If the controlling law is a statute, regulation or constitutional provision, it may be useful to begin by quoting the relevant portions of the law, followed by a systematic attempt to analyze how the law applies to the particular facts of the client's case. Your discussion must be integrated with all applicable case law (e.g., court opinions which have construed and applied the constitution or statute in question).

It is in the presentation and analysis of authority that the internal memorandum differs most markedly from the external memorandum. The purpose of the internal memorandum is to objectively explore the authority governing the issue, pointing out the weaknesses as well as the strengths of the client's position. Hence as to all opinions that you are analogizing, you should give *both* sets of arguments on whether the holding in the opinion is analogous to the client's case. The external memorandum, on the other hand, attempts to minimize the weaknesses of the client's position in an attempt to persuade the reader to make a favorable decision. This does not mean that you are free in an external memorandum to concentrate on your best known arguments while completely ignoring those which favor the opposing party. You should fully expect that your opponent will raise those arguments which most favor his/her client. Unless you anticipate and meet these arguments in your memorandum, you may find yourself surprised by an adverse decision.

5. *Conclusion.*

At the end of your analysis of each issue you should briefly summarize your analysis and state the conclusion which you have reached on the question or issue you have treated. In an internal memorandum, your conclusion will normally be phrased in terms of a prediction of the likely outcome should the issue be litigated, perhaps coupled with recommendations concerning the strategy which should be adopted in handling the case. In an external memorandum, your conclusion will be a simple statement requesting that the court or agency rule in favor of your client on the issue being treated.

6. *Table of Contents.*

It is a requirement of most appellate courts that each brief submitted to the court include a table of contents.[7] The table is normally placed at the very beginning of the brief and lists its major components together with the number of the page on which each component begins. Although it is usually not necessary to include a table of contents in a memorandum of law, it is often helpful to do so, particularly where the memorandum is relatively long and complex.

7. *Table of Authorities Cited.*

Another standard requirement for appellate briefs is the inclusion of a table of authorities cited.[8] The table is usually presented at the beginning of the brief, immediately following the table of contents. It consists of a list of each authority cited in the brief together with the number of the page in the text of the brief on which the authority is cited and discussed. The listing is broken down into categories, e.g., constitutional provisions, statutes, court opinions (listed alphabetically), treatises, etc. Like the table of contents, this is a useful device to incorporate into your *legal memorandum*, particularly where the memorandum is relatively long and complex.

8. *Summary of Issues and Conclusions.*

In a memorandum involving more than one issue, as noted above, you should include a summary of the issues and conclusions at the *beginning* of the memorandum. The issues should be repeated in the body of the memorandum, immediately preceding the presentation and analysis of the authority on that issue.

9. *Counteranalysis.*

As we emphasized above in our discussion of the analysis component of a memorandum, it is *critical* that you develop the skill of anticipating the arguments which your opponent is likely to raise on each issue. The failure to do this is one of the most common mistakes that students make. Ordinarily in both the internal and external memorandum, your treatment of the opponent's position would be incorporated into your own analysis of the issues. For an internal memorandum, however, you may find it useful, particularly in your early legal writing ventures, to include a *separate* counteranalysis component for each issue in your memorandum. This component should come immediately after your own analysis and before your conclusion on the issue. In it you should attempt to analyze the issue from the perspective of the opposing party. Assume, in fact, that *you* are representing the opposing party, and attempt to raise whatever arguments you can in favor of that position. As you become more accustomed to spotting the weaknesses in your own position and the strengths in your opponent's position, you may find it more convenient and more effective to simply incorporate the counteranalysis directly into the analysis component of the memorandum.

10. *Next Steps.*

This component is used in many internal memoranda. In the course of researching and analyzing an issue, you may become aware of a number of additional steps that need to be taken in the case. You may conclude, for example, that:

- the client must file a lawsuit within ten days to prevent the statute of limitations from running; or
- additional facts (which you attempt to specify) are needed in order to give a more secure prediction of what the answer to an issue will be;

● additional research is needed in related areas of law.

Each of these next steps should be listed in the memorandum.   While it is permissible to simply include them in your conclusion, it is often better to accord them a separate place in the memorandum.

The organization and structure of a legal memorandum will vary a great deal depending upon the complexity of the individual memorandum; there is no one structure which will be appropriate in every case.   The primary factor which will influence your choice of a structure will be the number of issues which you intend to treat in the memorandum.   In a relatively uncomplicated memorandum involving only a single issue, you would use a relatively simple structure involving only the first five of the ten memorandum components listed above.   The following illustration shows how these components should be organized in such a memorandum:

Office Memorandum

TO: [*supervisor*]

FR: [*your name*]

RE: [*subject of memorandum*]

DA: [*today's date*]   CASE NO. [   ]

ISSUE

[*State the issue being treated.*]

FACTS

[*State the facts of the client's case.*]

ANALYSIS

[*State and discuss the relevant authorities with counteranalysis.*]

CONCLUSION

[*State your conclusions and recommendations, if any, for further action in the case.*]

More often, however, the memorandum will involve at least two issues and perhaps more.   A clear presentation of your research and analysis in such a memorandum requires a somewhat more elaborate structure.   The following illustration shows how a multiple issue memorandum could be structured:

Office Memorandum

TO: [*supervisor*]

FR: [*your name*]

OFFICE MEMORANDUM—continued

OFFICE MEMORANDUM—continued

RE: [*subject of memorandum*]

DA: [*today's date*] CASE NO: [   ]

A. SUMMARY OF ISSUES AND CONCLUSIONS:

ISSUE I.

[*State the first issue.*]

CONCLUSION

[*Briefly summarize your conclusion as to the first issue.*]

ISSUE II.

[*State the second issue.*]

CONCLUSION

[*Briefly state your conclusion as to the second issue.*]

B. FACTS:

[*State the facts of the client's case.*]

C. ANALYSIS:

ISSUE I.

[*Restate the first issue.   Then discuss the various authorities you have identified, present the counteranalysis and state your conclusions as to this issue.*]

ISSUE II.

[*Restate the second issue.   Then discuss the various authorities you have identified, present the counteranalysis and state your conclusions as to this issue.*]

D. CONCLUSION:

[*Summarize your conclusions on both issues and state your recommendations.*]

E. NEXT STEPS

If the memorandum is even longer and more complex, you should include the table of contents and the table of authorities mentioned above.

REFERENCES

Appleman, *Approved Appellate Briefs* (1958).

Bishkind, *Simplify Legal Writing* (1975).

Copen, *Writing from a Legal Perspective* (1981).

Cooper, *Writing in Law Practice* (1963).

Cook, *Legal Drafting* (1951).

Dickerson, *The Fundamentals of Legal Drafting* (1965).

Gilmer, *Legal Research, Writing and Advocacy* (1978).

Rombauer, *Legal Problem Solving: Analysis, Research and Writing* (1973).

Statsky & Wernet, *Case Analysis and Fundamentals of Legal Writing* (1978).

Strunk & White, *Elements of Style* (1959).

U.S. Gov't. Printing Office, *Style Manual* (1973).

Weihofen, *Legal Writing Style* (1961).

White, *The Legal Imagination: Studies in the Nature of Legal Thought and Expression* (1973).

Wydick, *Plain English for Lawyers* (1979).

FOOTNOTES

1. Supra p. 34
2. Supra p. 118
3. Supra p. 17
4. Supra p. 41
5. Supra p. 50
6. Statsky, W., & Wernet, J., *Case Analysis and Fundamentals of Legal Writing*, pp. 396ff. (1977).
7. Supra p. 153
8. Supra p. 154

INDEX

†